CONSCIOUS QUESTIONS

CONSCIOUS QUESTIONS

The power to influence extraordinary results

NEO BERNAL

Conscious Questions
First edition in Spanish, Jul 2023
First English Edition, Nov 2024

© MASTER DRAGON LLC, 2024

Blog: https://medium.com/@jpbernalm
YouTube: https://www.youtube.com/channel/UCZiH8p-9Fw94RvgvDcuY4-Fg
LinkedIn: https://www.linkedin.com/in/neo-bernal

Written by: Juan Pablo Bernal
Editing and Layout: David Manangón
Cover Design: Marco Pérez
Published by: Marcel Verand

This book may not be reproduced in whole or in part, or incorporated into a computer system, or transmitted in any form or by any means, electronic, mechanical, photocopying, recording or otherwise, without the prior written permission of the author. Infringement of the aforementioned rights may constitute an intellectual property crime.

All rights reserved.

Interactivity With Maxi, Your Intelligent Reading Assistant

Throughout this book, you'll have access to Maxi, a specialized Artificial Intelligence ready to accompany you in your learning journey via WhatsApp. Trained with the in-depth knowledge found in these pages, Maxi provides you with an interactive reading experience.

You can ask it to:

• Dive deeper into any concept that piques your interest.

• Generate additional examples to help you better understand.

• Validate if you've understood an idea correctly.

• Summarize specific chapters or sections to ease your review.

• Or even present challenges and questions you face, whether at work or in your daily life.

Make the most of this unique tool to get the most out of your reading!

Content

Interactivity With Maxi, Your Intelligent Reading Assistant 7
Introduction 11
PART I | ELEVATE YOUR ABILITY TO CREATE CONSCIOUS QUESTIONS 17
Chapter 1 | Preparation 19
    1. Clear Objective 21
    2. Key Information 25
    3. Adaptation to the Audience 28
Chapter 2 | Formulation 31
    4. Positive Questions 34
    5. Impartial Questions 40
    6. Open-ended Questions 41
Chapter 3 | Platform 43
    7. Attention 46
    8. Connection 51
    9. Demonstration 55
Chapter 4 | Strengthening the Muscle 61
    Learn from your Questions 63
    Prepare your Interactions 68
    Consciously Evolve your Platform 73
    Week 6: Focus on spiritual understanding 83
    Week 7: Strengthen the correlation 85

Week 8: Use positive body language 87
Week 9: Use verbal cues 88
Week 10: Use reflective listening 90
Week 11: Master the art of interrupting 91
Week 12: Ask consciously 93

PART II | CONSCIOUS QUESTIONS IN EVERYDAY LIFE 95

Chapter 5 | Helping others 97
Reinforcing Values 99
Building Behaviors 106

Chapter 6 | Making Decisions 113
Choosing which Idea to Pursue 117
Choosing a Job 121
Choosing What to Study 124

Chapter 7 | Navigating Difficult Conversations 129
Conflicts 132
Poor Ways of Handling Conflicts 135
Constructive Ways to Manage Conflicts 136

Chapter 8 | Seeking Guidance from a Leader 143

Chapter 9 | Empowering Work Teams 153

Conclusion 159
About the Book's Structure 160
About the Framework 162

Acknowledgments 163

About the Author 165

This is Only the Beginning 167

Notes 169

Introduction

"The power of a question is the power to change everything."

—Tony Robbins

Indeed, one question changed everything. At the end of 2022 I was diagnosed with *Anxiety and Depression Disorder*, also known as Burnout. It was a strong blow to my ego, but above all to my health, not only physical, but also mental and emotional. Full of helplessness, I asked myself: "**What is this for?**" That led me to think only about the past, fueling my stress, and limiting my learning.

Part of my recovery therapy involved finding a new *hobby*, an activity that energized me, while cleansing myself of the stress toxins of everyday life. At first, I thought about sports and social coexistence. I love people, but I also love being alone. I remembered that spending time with people requires additional use of energy, while spending time alone recharges me. That's why I love reading and meditating.

One day, reflecting on the *hobby*, I asked myself: "**Why** did this happen to me?", and that was when I had the understanding, the clarity necessary to choose something that brings together a good number of things that energize me. I got sick like this to write my first book, this book. Now, with my being back in creative mode, I asked myself "**what am I writing about**?"

This question led me to review my entire working life. I remembered that during more than twenty years of professional career, multiple defects and opportunities for improvement have been pointed out to me, on which I have worked hard. However, I have also received a recognition, unison and constant, regardless of the environment, team or challenge in which I participate: "Neo makes things happen." Reflecting on this led me to understand that questions were the fundamental pillar of that power. And, furthermore, I was able to decode what was special and unique in my questions, since many recognized that they managed to mobilize people in a way that few leaders had managed to do. I called these types of questions **Conscious Questions**.

Before we move forward, I want to apologize for my mistakes as a first-time writer and thank you for considering reading the book. Above all, I want you to find an ultimate tool to take your leadership style to the next level. I hope that you can use **Conscious Questions** to help others, as well as yourself, achieve extraordinary results.

Several of these concepts are present in the title and subtitle of the book, and about them I would like to suggest some key distinctions. These are relevant to ensure that we are looking in the same direction when reading it.

1. Ask: Search deep. Etymological definitions[1] relate the word "question" to a search, a trial or survey. But not only that, they also suggest that this search is done deep down, in the depths.

2. Consciousness: Human capacity to feel at *one with everyone and everything*[2]. Unlike studies that consider consciousness as a state of mind, consciousness is a spiritual state derived from the connection with all living beings.

3. Power: Ability to act to achieve a specific objective. There is the idea of power derived from authority and the power of a superhero. Today I believe in the power that comes from dynamic energy, movement, action.

4. Influence: Add value with integrity[3]. Far from the intention to manipulate, influencing is our ability to give others the best of ourselves.

5. Extraordinary results: Product that significantly exceeds expectations. Success beyond success.

Putting everything together, we have the elements to formulate a main definition. *A* **Conscious Question** *is one that is created deliberately and focused. It is open, impartial, positive and adapted to the audience. Additionally, it has the power to generate deep and actionable reflections that lead to extraordinary results.*

Now, why ask? Typically, we ask questions to seek information, clarify, or explore new ideas, as detailed below:

1. Search for information: By asking questions, we can gather information and learn about new topics.

2. Clarify our knowledge: Asking questions can help us better understand a concept, idea or hypothesis.

3. Explore new ideas: Asking questions allows us to consider different perspectives and explore new alternatives, which can lead to new insights.

And, more specifically, why ask **Conscious Questions**? To enjoy the value proposition of this book: *Influencing extraordinary results*. But how to achieve it? After understanding and decoding the unique aspects of a **Conscious Question**, I established a *framework* with nine distinctive features that I classified into three dimensions: **Preparation, Formulation**, and **Platform**; as I present in *figure 1*. As you will see, they are obvious and common-sense features; however, not necessarily common practice.

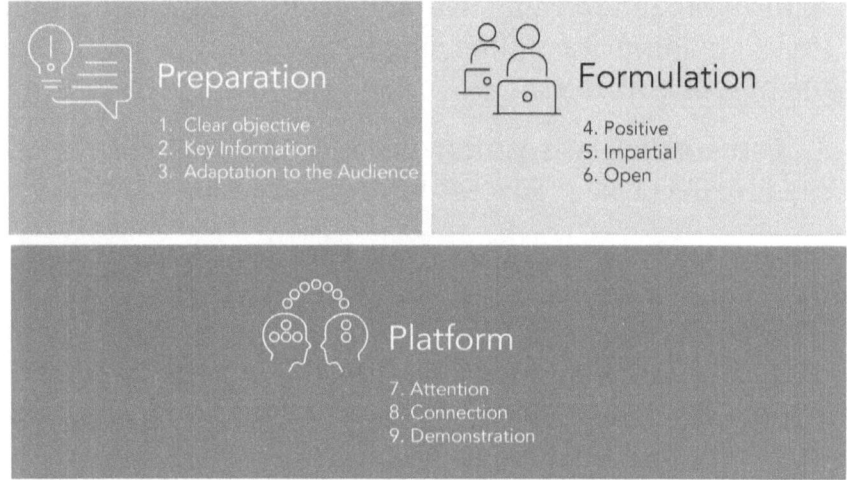

Figure 1: Framework to build Conscious Questions

With the help of this *framework*, you will be able to refine your current questions and create new questions that change everything. To learn how to do this, you will be able to navigate the book between its two general parts. In the first, you will find the theoretical foundations of the *framework* and you will have a guide to become a master of masters. In the second part, you will see practical applications for multiple situations in daily life.

Let's delve below into the theoretical principles and practical elements of each of the features that make **Conscious Questions** unique and powerful.

PART I

ELEVATE YOUR ABILITY TO CREATE CONSCIOUS QUESTIONS

In the following chapters we will go through, feature by feature, the *framework* necessary to create **Conscious Questions**. We will build the entire Conceptual Framework and establish routines that will lead you to mastery in the subject.

CHAPTER 1

Preparation

«Preparation is not something that is done once and then forgotten;
it is a constant process that leads to success."

—*Zig Ziglar*

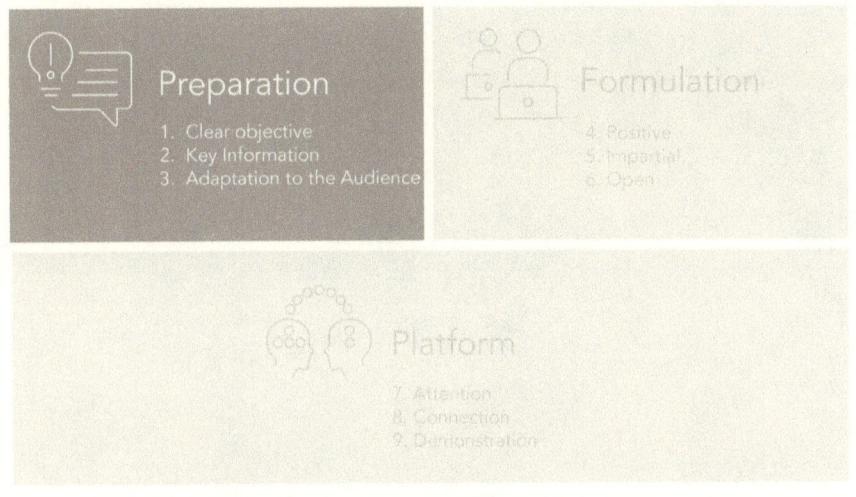

Figure 2: Preparation Dimension for Conscious Questions

Sometimes we have the possibility of structuring a work session, a meeting or any other event with someone in advance, which gives us the possibility of pre-designing some questions. Although there are techniques such as the perspective game[4] to explore possible flows of a conversation, the usual thing is that, in an authentic conversation, we must create most questions live. A well-prepared **Conscious Question** considers: *clear objectives, key information and adaptation to the audience.* Let's explore each of these features.

1. Clear Objective

Start with a clear goal in mind. What do you hope to achieve by asking that question? Answering this will help you create intentional and relevant questions. Sometimes the answer is easy, but other times you will surely have to investigate a little more, with yourself or with your interlocutor, to identify the objective of your **Conscious Question**. *Dr. Richard Paul*[5] did a study on the *Socratic Method* and classified the questions into six categories:

1. Clarifying

2. Reasoning and arguing

3. Examining assumptions

4. Investigating causes and consequences

5. Seeking the origin of ideas

6. Exploring perspectives and viewpoints.

These types of questions have been useful to me to clarify the objective I want to pursue when asking a **Conscious Question**:

1. Clarifying:

- What do you mean with …?
- Could you explain… in another way?
- What do you think is the most important aspect of…?
- Why do you say that…?
- How does this relate to what we were talking about…?
- Could you give an example of…?
- What do we know about…?

2. Reasoning and arguing:

- Why happens …?
- How do you know that…?
- Could you teach me …?
- Why do you think… it's true?
- What other information would we need to know if… it is true?
- What leads you to think that…?
- Is there any reason to doubt…?
- How could we know if… it's true?

3. Examining assumptions:

- How did you come to assume that...?
- What other things can we assume about...?
- Why would anyone assume that...?

4. Investigating causes and consequences:

- What would happen if...?
- What would be the consequences of...?
- How would it influence... on...?
- What does it imply that...?
- What else would happen if it were true that...?

5. Seeking the origin of ideas:

- Where does that idea come from...?
- Do you think your opinion about... is influenced by something or someone?
- What makes you think like that about...?

6. Exploring perspectives and viewpoints:

- How else could we see...?
- What other point of view could we take about...?
- How would you (another group) respond to the statement about...?
- What objections to... would you (another group) make?
- What would you say about... someone who thought (another way of thinking)?

Conscious Questions

Let's now explore the power of asking questions when the objective is already clear. In high-performance work teams there are usually many different ideas, since they tend to be made up of extremely bright people. Such an environment can be challenging, because great intellectual ability is often accompanied by high egos, egos that usually do not like to lose. Asking questions with the aim of appealing to the emotional side over the rational, for example, is usually a powerful tool, since, if you allow such a team to understand and listen to how their colleagues feel, it usually helps them empathize and converge more quickly. I remember an anecdote in which the president of a company managed to align his management team thanks to posing a **Conscious Question** that had a supremely clear objective.

I was meeting with the president and vice presidents of a company. We were reviewing success stories and lessons learned from other organizational transformations at scale. The president had already convinced himself that adopting adaptive management was the next step for the company he commanded; However, his team only had two executives on board, seven were in a neutral zone and three openly declared themselves opponents of the idea. In the middle of the session, the president asked me, along with my other colleagues, to let them have a private conversation. We agreed immediately and gave them their space. A few minutes later they invited us back into the room and we were informed that they were ready to begin their transformation journey.

A couple of days later, we asked the president if it was possible to know what had happened in his private space. «I asked each member of my team to answer one question: "How do you feel about making this transformation and why?" At the end of the round, I also shared my own emotions with the team. In a very natural and empathetic way, I felt like I could genuinely understand them all, and I didn't see right or wrong positions, just different points of view on the same situation. From my heart I told them that I understood them, that if it were a job that I could do alone, it would not be so relevant that everyone was willing to do it. I told them that at that moment, more than ever, we needed to be a solid team, not because we all thought the same, but because we were all willing to support each other and correct course, if necessary. In the end, together we made the decision to move forward.

A **Conscious Question** requires a clear objective. When it is not clear enough, we can use questions, such as those presented by *Dr. Richard Paul*, to clear the air and see more clearly where to direct the efforts of the central questions.

2. Key Information

Identify the key information you need to achieve the objective of the question. What do you need to know to make this deliberate and focused? Make a list of these key pieces of information and use them to guide the creation of your questions. Information can have multiple origins and characteristics depending on the context. Therefore, I usually use a generic inquiry technique about:

1. the present

2. the past

3. possible futures

Years ago, I had a business with a couple of other people, which operated from my mother's house. One afternoon, my grandmother knocked on my door, and a very elegant man showed up. It was a representative of one of the government agencies, he was looking for more information about my business. I invited him in, and we talked for a while. I'm going to refer to him as *Mr. Diego*.

— [...]

— Good afternoon. What do I owe the honor of your visit, Mr. Diego?

— We received an alert. There are a large number of deposits from different parts of the country directed to your account. The quantity and amounts grow very quickly, it is suspicious. Many of the locations from which the transfers come are places marked as areas prone to terrorist financing activities.

— I understand. We are happy about the accelerated growth of the business; However, this situation you mention also alerts me. Please could you tell me a little more? —I responded evenly.

—You should know that many national companies also receive payments that include these red zones. Most are corporations or other types of companies, but they have been incorporated and have been operating for several years. In your case, we see that you operate using the national identification number, without a legal figure, that makes your operation more formal.

—Yes, it seems that you are just reading my mind. Have you had similar situations before?

—Yes, of course, and more frequently than you imagine.

—Well, I hope there are more people undertaking things and fewer wanting to do inappropriate things. By the way, what has happened in cases where they have actually found situations outside the law?

—There are cases where the business is within the legal framework, but its clients use it as a channel for illicit purposes. In others, it is the company that acts illegally —said Mr. Diego.

—Surely there must be everything. And what has happened before in cases where everything is within the parameters expected by your agency? —I continued investigating.

—It has its nuances —he told me with more confidence—. I have seen companies that, due to the nature of their activity, must be regulated and monitored by the corresponding agency, not necessarily the one that I represent. Other organizations do not fit into the above group, but must still provide us with information whenever required, typically every six to twelve months.

—Wow, this is all a new world for me. And with the information you already have about my business, what would be a good scenario once your visit is over?

—It depends on what we call "good scenario". If you mean that you can continue with your business, we will probably require data from the operation on a regular basis, but I don't think we will reach a level of regulation and surveillance. Although we should validate this hypothesis in the detailed review that we need to do.

—I think it's great. You are a highly qualified professional, Mr. Diego. Tell me now, what is that detailed review about and how can we help make it successful?

—[...]

You can't imagine how terrified I felt; However, looking back, the relevant information I was able to gather during the talk, exploring the present, the past and the future, not only helped me create a better professional and emotional connection with the agent, but also allowed me to be better prepared, both to ask and to answer.

Some typical questions look like this:

- **Present:** How would you summarize what is happening? How do you feel today about this situation or person? What are the facts?

- **Past:** What have you tried before? What do you think moved you to act the way you did? What do you think moved them to do what they did?

- **Future:** What would you like to happen? What would the ideal world look like? How would you like to feel independent of what happens?

Thus, when we lack the minimum information, we need to achieve the objective of the **Conscious Question** that we are preparing, to find it, we can explore the present, the past and the future during the conversation.

3. Adaptation to the Audience

Think about your audience. Who are you going to ask these questions and what do they know about the topic in question? Tailor the questions to your audience, making sure they are appropriate for their level of knowledge and understanding.

My birthday is one day after my maternal grandmother's. On one occasion we had the celebration together and opened the gifts at the same time. When I uncovered the virtual reality glasses they gave me, my grandmother asked "so what is that?" My quick and "intelligent" response was: "they are virtual reality glasses." As I responded, I heard myself say something that could be from a specialized technical domain. Then I added: "Granny, it's like a computer or a cell phone, which is used like a helmet, and it looks so real that that's why it's called virtual reality. Come, I'll show you".

It's not about judging whether someone knows or understands more or less than us, it's about being empathetic with the vocabulary we use, since we could be the ones on the side with less technical mastery. For example, one afternoon in the first session with my psychologist, during the conversation, he talked about "framing." My mind began to spin, first I thought of a camera, then of my dad's works of art. When no reference helped me understand, I interrupted and asked what framing meant in the context of therapy. So, my psychologist adapted his technical language a little more to help me stay connected to him.

I was accompanying the preparation process to launch a business unit following adaptive management practices. I had a work session with the leader of one of the teams that was part of the unit. In his work map, the main business results could begin to be captured in the twelfth month of the team's operation. After investigating, understanding and confirming his logic, I was very excited and said: "Based on your plan, what would you need so that we can capture value from the first month of operation instead of the twelfth month?" At first, he was defensive, saying that if it were that easy, he would have designed the plan that way. After a couple of arguments, he asked me how to do it, and then I had the opportunity to explain the concept of *Walking Skeleton*[6] to him, its relationship with a *Minimum Viable Product*[7], and some of the principles that would help us adjust the plan and, of course, aspire to move the needle of the business much faster. If in my provocative question I had mentioned the technical concept without further context or without translating it into what might be interesting to him (faster results), there was a chance that the conversation would have been more challenging, not because he wasn't a brilliant person, but because he was just beginning his learning path about adaptive management.

Adaptation can also have a time and space feature. There are places and times that may be more convenient to ask certain questions. Maybe you can remember that work session when you wish you hadn't asked a question, but you did. That question that marked a before and after, only because it was not the time to ask it. Surely you had a clear objective and the necessary information, but it was neither the time nor the place.

The following questions can serve as training for your mental process of adapting the form, time and space to consciously ask:

1. Is this question appropriate for the audience's level of knowledge and understanding?

2. Is this question appropriate, given the audience's current emotional state or the topic being discussed?

3. Is this question likely to offend or make any audience member uncomfortable?

4. Is this question sensitive to the current social, political or economic climate?

The third element to *Prepare* a **Conscious Question** invites us to reflect on the "who", the "when" and the "where", which leads us to enhance our empathy through consciously choosing our vocabulary, the moment and the place.

Preparation stage leads us to enhance skills that, used both proactively and reactively, provide us with the key inputs to create **Conscious Questions.**

The *Formulation* phase will give us a perspective on what those inputs look like converted into the final product. Let's explore the next three distinctive features.

CHAPTER 2

Formulation

"It is not the answer that illuminates, but the question."

—*Eugene Ionesco*

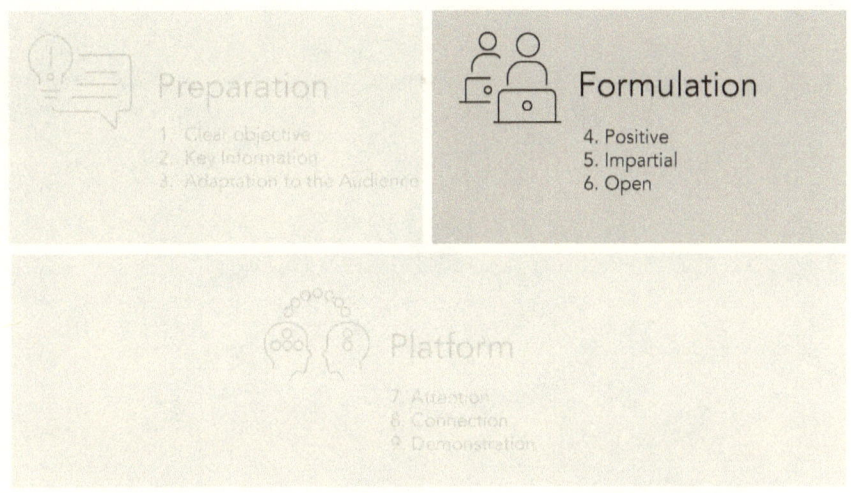

Figure 3: Formulation Dimension for Conscious Questions

As in *Preparation*, it may be that we have time to pre-write our questions, reviewing in detail the key aspects of the *Formulation*: that they be **positive, impartial** and **open**. However, what is usually more natural is that we must use these criteria in the middle of the conversation. To achieve this level of mastery only one thing is required: practice. **Positive questions** are those that exhibit five wise mindsets: *The Empath, the Explorer, the Innovator, the Navigator, and the Activator.* **Impartial questions** are those free of prejudice, avoid subjective considerations and favoritism, and focus on the objective part of the facts. **Open-ended questions,** on the other hand, invite debate by avoiding bias in possible yes or no, or multiple-choice answers.

To better mark the difference between impartial and open questions, let's think about an antonym of the former, leading questions. These are intended to manipulate the conversation and often lead to a specific answer, while open-ended questions are intended to encourage elaboration and exploration of the topic. Let's now review each of the aspects to formulate **Conscious Questions**.

4. Positive Questions

Shirzad Chamine, a professor at Stanford and Yale business schools, has coached senior executives at most *Fortune 500 companies*, and has coached hundreds of *CEOs* and their teams. He has used the concept of *Positive Intelligence*[8] *as the basis of his coaching and training* sessions for years. Their studies demonstrate that, while Intelligence Quotient (*IQ*) and Emotional Quotient (*EQ*) contribute to an individual's maximum potential, it is the Positivity Quotient (*PQ*) that determines how much of that potential can actually be achieved. Like most powerful things, *PQ* is easy to understand on an intellectual level; however, mastering it requires attention and practice.

Professor *Chamine* defines *Positive Intelligence* as a person's ability to keep their mind as a friend, acting in its best interest. This ability is developed through strengthening what he calls the *Sages* and weakening the *Saboteurs*.

Before moving forward with these concepts, let's pause and think about an everyday situation. Surely you remember someone saying something like: "My God, **what** is this happening to me for?", or in contrast: "**why** is this happening to me?". Both are valuable questions, one exploring the past and the other the future. However, the first sounds like a reflection with a possible bias of disappointment or regret, while the second shows an openness to new possibilities. The first manifests one of the nine **Saboteurs**, *the Victim*; the second exhibits one of the five **Sages**, *the Explorer*.

The Saboteurs

As you will see, *Saboteurs* are useful mental programs in specific moments and circumstances. However, they become harmful when they take control of our interactions on a regular basis, and not us who consciously use them in special cases.

0. The Judge: He is the *master saboteur*, who contains in himself the nine accomplice *saboteurs*. *The Judge* constantly forces you to find fault in yourself, in others, in conditions and circumstances. It tends to generate a lot of your anxiety, stress, anger, disappointment, shame, regret and guilt. The questions *the Judge* asks often contain variations of: "What is wrong with me?" "What is wrong with you?" "What is wrong with this situation?" "What is wrong with this result?"

1. The Perfectionist: Needs extreme order and organization. It generates a lot of anxiety, tension and frustration in you and others around you, consuming everyone's energy to try to reach a level of perfection that is not necessary. Their typical questions include: "And why did we fail if I told you how to do it flawlessly?" "What can we do to avoid failing again?" "Can someone explain to me why this is taking longer than expected?" "What should we do to make it perfect?"

2. The Pleaser: It leads you to try to gain acceptance and affection by constantly helping, pleasing, rescuing or flattering others. It makes you lose sight of your own needs and, as a result, makes you resentful of others. It also encourages others to depend too much on you. Your comments may sound like: "What can we do to make the president happy?" "What did the boss say he wanted?" "Would it be better to remove this to avoid arguments?" "Don't you think he's ungrateful?"

3. The *Hyper-achiever*: It makes you depend on high performance and constant achievements to have self-respect and self-validation. You tend to focus only on external success, giving little consideration to the internal aspects of happiness, such as personal values. Typically, it generates unsustainable *workaholism tendencies* (work addiction) and causes a disconnection with deeper emotional needs. This *saboteur* usually leads us to ask questions like: "Why are we wasting time with these workshops on leadership and emotional management?"

"Can we better use our time focusing on producing business results?" "Why are we spending the entire team's time on those retrospective sessions?"

4. The Victim: He wants you to feel emotional and temperamental as a way to gain attention and affection. The result is an extreme concentration on internal feelings, especially painful ones, and can often lead to a martyr's attitude. The consequences are that you waste your mental and emotional energy, and others feel frustrated, helpless or guilty for not being able to make you happy for a long time. *The Victim l*eads us to ask things like: "But why do I always get the most difficult projects?" "Are you calling me to tell me another problem?" "Who made this decision?"

5. The Hyperrational: Creates an intense and exclusive focus on rationally processing everything, including relationships. It makes you impatient with people's emotions and considers them unworthy of much time or consideration. When you are under the influence of the *Hyperrational*, you may be perceived as cold, distant, or intellectually arrogant. It limits your depth and flexibility in work or personal relationships and intimidates less analytical people. Its questions may look like: "Can we get to the point?" "How about we skip the whole soap opera?" "But what else do they want?" "Could you bring me actionable discussions?"

6. The Hypervigilant: It makes you feel intense and continuous anxiety about all the dangers around you and what could go wrong. It puts you on constant alert and affects your rest. It causes a lot of continuous stress that wears down you and others. You know a *Hypervigilant* when you hear things like: "Have we already exhaustively identified all the risks and their mitigations?" "And how come we didn't anticipate this situation?" "What do we do to avoid having more problems until delivery?"

7. The Tireless: Is constantly seeking greater excitement in the next activity or through perpetual busyness. It doesn't allow you to feel much peace or satisfaction with your current activity. It provides you with an endless stream of distractions that make you lose focus on the things and relationships that really matter. Other people find it difficult to keep up with the person ruled by *the Tireless* mindset and often feel distanced from them. This one, ask things like: "What time can we see this finished today?" "Does everyone have homework, so people aren't wasting their time?" "What else can we do to keep people fully occupied?"

8. The Controller: It is based on the anxious need to take charge, control situations and subject people's actions to your will. It generates a lot of anxiety and impatience when this is not possible. In the *Controller's* worldview, you either have control or you don't. Although the *Controller* allows you to obtain short-term results, in the long term it generates resentment in others and prevents them from exercising and developing their own abilities to the fullest. Its questions look like this: "What time can we see this before the executive committee?" "How many times have I told you not to do that like that?" "Why are we spending time on that?"

9. The Avoider: It focuses you on the positive and the pleasant in an extreme way, it avoids difficult and unpleasant questions and conflicts. It leads to habits of procrastination and conflict avoidance, which translate into collateral damage in relationships and cause delays in the execution of initiatives. *The Avoider* asks things like: "What could we do that is within our reach, so we don't have to take this to the *holding company*?" «Can we think of another alternative, since the *CEO has never liked this path*? » "How about we keep a low profile with this?"

The Sages

While the *Saboteurs* represent our internal enemies when they take control of our interactions, the *Sages* represent the most prudent and wise part.

1. The Empath: It makes you feel and show appreciation, compassion and forgiveness, both towards yourself and others. Normally, we are harassed by our own *Judge* and that of others, draining energy from everyone in their path. Empathy helps us recharge the emotional reserves necessary to address everyday challenges. You'll be displaying your *Empathic Sage* with questions like: "How do you feel about the progress you've made so far?" "What obstacles or challenges do you have right now?" "What can I do to help you achieve your goals?" «What do you think of the comments we received from the client?» "What do they need from me to be successful?"

2. The Explorer: Like children, *the Explorer* provides energy through his great curiosity and fascination with discovery. It's an energizing mindset, even in crisis situations. Some common questions are: "What things did we not know that we didn't know?" "What would be the main levers that we will be highlighting in three years as those that made a big difference today?" "What new opportunities is this loss showing us?"

3. The Innovator: His power is based on thinking and acting without boxes, without assumptions. It releases energy, as it questions processes and habits to make new realities possible. While *the Explorer* discovers things that already exist, *the Innovator* creates them. We will hear it asking: "What could we achieve if the main limitations we have today did not exist?" "How do you imagine this solution in an ideal world?" "What habits should we change to overcome this goal that seems impossible today?"

4. The Navigator: Your power is based on the ability to choose between different paths and alternatives, based on your internal compass. This is configured with the deepest values, the purpose and meaning of life. Navigating with such a compass creates an accumulation of decisions, creating a sense of fulfillment from living a life aligned with the highest ideals and principles. *The Navigator* often uses questions like: "What is most valuable to you, regardless of the outcome?" "How much do you feel you are honoring your values in this situation?" "What do you consider to be the underlying motivations or reasons behind this?" "What would make you proud of your performance regardless of the result?"

5. The Activator: It is useful when there is a clear path of action to take. Unlike the *Hyper-achiever*, who seeks results above all else, or t*he Hyperrational*, who ignores emotional cues, or *the Victim*, who invests a lot of energy worrying about what can go wrong, the *Activator's power* comes from his ability to act without being distracted by *Saboteurs*. He knows how to jump into action with an appropriate balance between holistic vision and laser focus. It has a holistic approach because it considers itself, others, its emotions, values, purpose and principles. And he has laser focus because he directs all his mental and emotional energy into pure action. You will see an *Activator* when you hear: "What are the priorities you are focused on this cycle?" "Do you have in mind the things we should put all our energy into right now?" "What could you stop doing that is not generating value right now?"

The first distinctive feature to ask **Conscious Questions** is that they are Positive. This characteristic requires enhancing our **Positive Intelligence**, withdrawing energy from the nine *Sabotaging Mindsets* and refocusing it on the five *Sages Mindsets*.

5. Impartial Questions

Avoid leading questions. These are questions that suggest a specific answer or that sway the respondent toward a specific point of view. Try to create neutral and unbiased questions that allow for sincere and authentic answers.

Leading questions guide the conversation in a certain direction, suggesting a specific answer. They usually begin with words like: "Don't you think...?", "Aren't you...?", or "Wouldn't you...?" Leading questions are often used to manipulate the conversation.

Imagine a straight line, in which on the right end you have the impartial questions and on the left the leading questions; The objective we pursue is to create questions that tend to the right. Let's look at some examples that give color to the line you imagined.

Leading	Impartial
1. Don't you think it's time for a change in leadership?	1. What do you think of the current leadership?
2. Does it true that the other candidate has a history of dishonesty?	2. Can you tell me about the other candidate's record?
3. Don't you agree that this policy is the only solution to the problem?	3. What are the possible solutions to the problem being discussed?
4. Isn't it clear that the company's results have suffered under the current management?	4. How would you assess the company's results under the current management?
5. Don't you think this proposal is too risky?	5. What are the potential risks associated with this proposal?

Figure 4: Comparison of leading and impartial questions

Impartiality is the second distinguishing feature of asking Conscious Questions. An impartial question leads to a more authentic conversation to the extent that it avoids tilting it in a direction biased by the questioner.

6. Open-ended Questions

Avoid closed questions. Open-ended questions invite debate and allow for a wide range of responses, while closed-ended, yes/no or multiple-choice questions tend to limit the depth of conversation.

Open-ended questions allow the person questioned to give a more elaborate answer. They are not specific, and the conversation is left open so that the person being asked can develop their thoughts and opinions. They usually begin with words like "what," "which," "how," and "why." Open-ended questions are widely used in research, interviews and conversations to encourage a person to share their thoughts, feelings and ideas.

On the opposite side we have closed questions. They are those that restrict the options between which the recipient will have to respond, who will only have to choose between some of them. The following examples better illustrate the nuance between an open and closed question.

Closed	Open
1. Do you want to quit your job?	1. How do you feel about your job?
2. Do you prefer sweet or salty foods?	2. Can you tell me about your favorite foods and any restrictions you have?
3. Are you liberal or conservative?	3. What opinion do you have about politics?

Closed	**Open**
4. How many years of experience do you have in this field?	4. What is your work experience and how did you end up in your current role?
5. Do you like working in agile environments or do you prefer traditional ones?	5. Why would you choose to work with an agile management style over a more traditional one?

Figure 5: Comparison of closed and open-ended questions

Naturally, in everyday contexts we also need closed questions. Maybe you don't want to spark a whole debate about dietary restrictions when you just want to know if the person prefers sweet over salty. The key is to be aware, knowing the objective we are pursuing with the question and adapting it to the audience and the situation. In other words, you don't have to bring out your arsenal of Open-ended Conscious Questions when you are cooking with your partner.

This third distinctive feature for formulating Conscious Questions is probably the one that professionals who use questions as part of the core of their activity are most aware of. An open-ended question is one that invites debate, avoiding suggesting specific alternatives as answers.

So far, we have explored the first two blocks of the framework, which group together six of the nine distinctive features of a Conscious Question. The three features of the Preparation phase give us the inputs, and the three features of the Formulation phase show us the characteristics of the finished product. Now, I invite you to delve into the third block that brings together the three final features that show us how we convert inputs into the product.

CHAPTER 3

Platform

«There is no better demonstration of interest than listen carefully and connect with the reality of the interlocutor.

—*Roy T. Bennett*

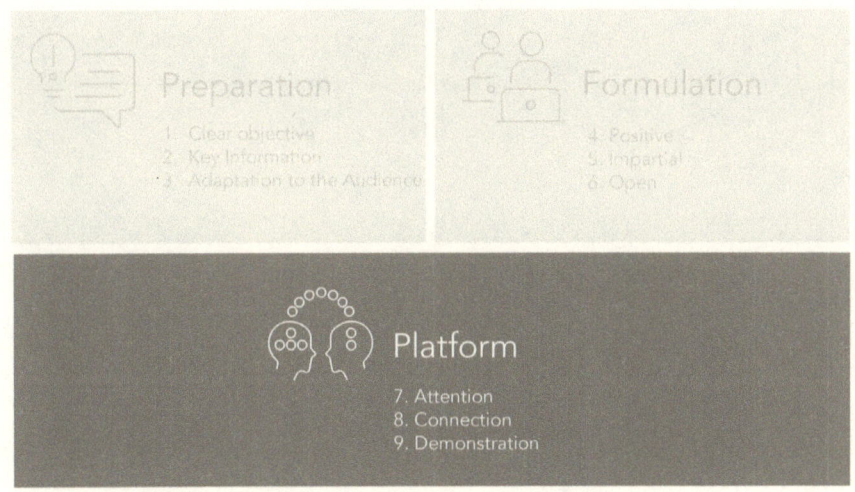

Figure 6: Platform Dimension for Conscious Questions

Let's look at the *framework* again, inspired by a factory. In the *Preparation* stage, the inputs are arranged; In *Formulation* the product is created and delivered; and the *Platform* is all the machinery through which inputs *flow*, the product is built and released. Preparation and Formulation are the "What" and the *Platform* is the "How". And it is this "How" that guarantees the distinctive touch of power. The inputs may be good, but without the appropriate Platform, without a powerful "How", the product could be defective and, therefore, generate less impactful experiences. So how to do it? The most powerful way to ask **Conscious Questions** is to always be aware, which requires mainly three skills: **being attentive,** present and focused; **connect with the interlocutor,** reflecting and understanding their perspective and emotions; and **demonstrate genuine interest** in the conversation and the responses received.

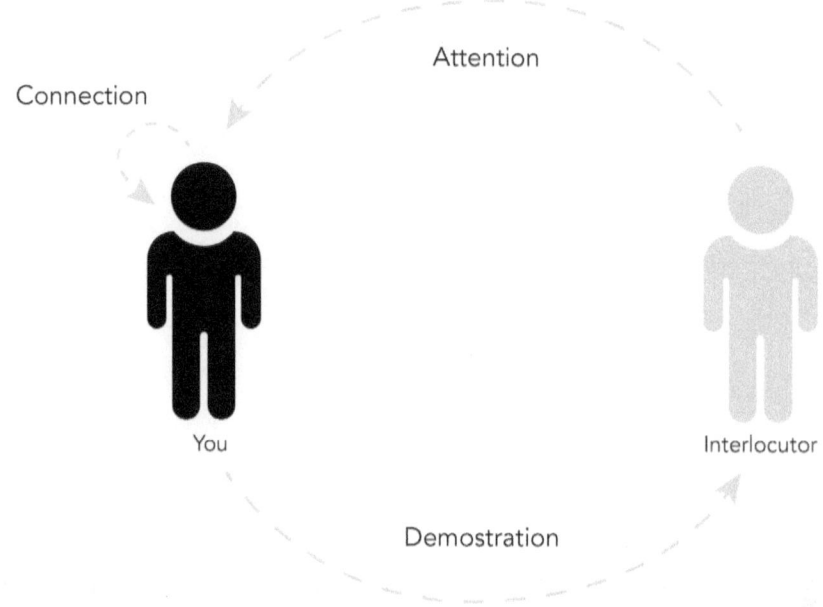

Figure 7: Process in the Platform Dimension: Attention, Connection and Demostration

7. Attention

One of the most important skills in creating **Conscious Questions** is paying full attention to the person we are talking to. This means being totally focused on the present moment. By doing this we are able to capture valuable information and exquisite details (see feature 2, *Key Information*) that go beyond words, such as bodily or nonverbal signals. The more and better privileged data, the better we can understand the perspectives and emotions of the interlocutor, as we will see in the *Connection feature*. Paying full attention is like having the radio station tuned in well in the car. If we do not choose the correct frequency, we will hear noise, the information will be incomplete and it will be very difficult for us to follow whatever they are transmitting, or even understand what it is about.

Similarly, when we do not pay attention adequately, we could risk generating noise and misunderstandings that will surely lead to a disconnection with the audience. For example, imagine you are in a work meeting and your mind is somewhere else or you are *multitasking*. You won't be fully listening to your colleagues, and you'll miss important information. All this lack of *Attention* could lead to confusion, rework and frustration.

When we pay *attention*, we are tuning into elements, both verbal and nonverbal. Research suggests that nonverbal communication can account for a high percentage of a message's meaning[9]. To find more meaning in nonverbal elements, we can be aware of things like facial expressions, body language, tone of voice, gestures, and proximity.

Facial expressions can convey a wide range of emotions, such as happiness, sadness, anger, or surprise. For example, a smile can imply happiness, while a frown can mean worry or frustration.

Body language can communicate emotions and attitudes, such as confidence, uncertainty or discomfort. For example, standing up straight and maintaining eye contact may denote confidence; while slouching and avoiding eye contact may signal uncertainty or discomfort.

The tone of voice can show emotions and attitudes, such as excitement, sarcasm, or anger. For example, a high-pitched, cheerful tone may signal enthusiasm, while a monotone or sarcastic tone may imply lack of interest or disapproval.

Gestures can indicate meaning and emphasis, such as pointing, nodding, or shaking your head. For example, nodding your head can mean agreement or understanding, while shaking your head can suggest disagreement or disbelief.

Proximity can convey intimacy, dominance, or submission. For example, being close to someone can show intimacy or dominance, while being far away can communicate distance or submission.

It is important to pay *attention* to verbal and nonverbal cues during communication, as both contribute to the meaning of a message. Being aware, especially of nonverbal communication, can help you understand others better and communicate more effectively.

To increase your ability to pay attention you can consider three practices:

- Reduce or eliminate distractors
- Avoid the temptation of *multitasking*
- Practice meditation

Eliminate distractors

Before we delete them, let's do a scan. Let's try to list possible distractors thinking about two different illustrative scenarios: an in-person work session in the office, and a virtual one from home. Let's say that in the office we are in a meeting room, because if it were in the cafeteria or another open space, the list of distractors would probably be longer. We will have distractors, such as our own cell phone or smart watch, or that of other participants; the living room clock (the kind that rings like horror movie bells); If the room has glass walls, someone may walk by and say hello, or enter the room unexpectedly; The power could go out while a person is presenting, then the laptop battery will run out, just to name a few. Which of these distractors are under your control and could you eliminate them? Well, silencing the cell phone and/or placing it with the screen facing the table could help, turning off the clock notifications, turning your back to the glass wall, or connecting the laptop to the power supply, etc.

Now, imagine that we are having a meeting remotely from home. What distractors come to mind? Your partner passes by and winks at you, there is a call from the porter's lodge, your daughter has a class change, your pet barks, your grandmother raises her voice to get your mother's attention, they begin to repair the street, your neighbors express their joy with loud music, among other possible distractions. Think about your own distracting situations from home, what can you do to eliminate or mitigate them? What is under your control?

Avoid multitasking

Multitasking "at the same time" is a type of distraction. I decided to put it as a separate category because of the strong impact it has on our productivity. That is to say, it is one thing to be distracted by someone's greeting for a few moments, and another is that, while I am in a meeting, I get caught up in a parallel conversation in the chat or by email, or worse still, to be connected in two or three meetings at the same time. Several studies have shown the negative impact of *multitasking* on productivity. A study conducted by the *American Psychological Association* concluded that multitasking reduces productivity by up to 40 %. Another study published in the International *Journal of Information Management* reported that multitasking can increase the time needed to complete tasks by up to 25 %. *The Journal of Experimental Psychology* found that switching from one task to another can increase the time it takes to complete tasks by up to 50 %. Finally, the *University of California* published that multitasking could reduce the quality of work and increase the likelihood of making mistakes. These studies show that, instead of making us more effective, *multitasking* reduces our productivity, increases the time it takes us to complete tasks, and is a source of errors and detriment to the quality of our work.

Now, how to avoid it? There is no magic recipe, you must make the decision and do it. If you are a single-task person, congratulations! If not, I invite you to try it for a week and validate the studies and statistics firsthand.

Meditating

In recent years, this practice has become quite common. We hear about meditations for sleep, for exercise, posture and breathing. There are also digital companies that have created apps to assist meditation, and that achieve such popularity that they have already achieved "unicorn" valuations, that is, they are worth more than a billion dollars, such as the *apps*: *Calm* or *Innergy* (my favorite), to mention the most popular.

Since I was a child, I have been very restless with meditation, and I have tried multiple techniques. However, it was in 2003, while living in Cali, Colombia, that I learned about the technique that to this day remains the most powerful and universal I have experienced. It is called *Meditation on light or Meditation of the Science of Spirituality*. I described this meditation technique for executives in the article *How to Develop Our Maximum Potential*[10]. You can also find official instructions on the SOS.org page[11]. The founder of the *Science of Spirituality, Sant Rajinder,* is also a renowned scientist, businessman and author. He has written numerous books on how to incorporate meditation into daily life, deriving multiple benefits, not only in the physical sphere, but also in the mental, emotional and, above all, spiritual. If you want to delve deeper into this topic, I recommend two of his books: *Inner and Outer Peace through Meditation and Detox the Mind.*

Hundreds of studies have demonstrated in recent years the benefits of meditation, especially in the mental area. Most agree that meditation improves focus, attention and concentration; improves cognitive performance and memory; reduces symptoms of anxiety and depression; improves resilience and coping skills; reduces symptoms of ADHD and other attention-related disorders.

If you want to check the impact of meditation on your *Attention*, a good way is to practice it for seven days, every day, at the same time and place. For example, you get up, freshen your face, sit in a chair for five minutes and follow the instructions I recommended in the article. At night, just before going to bed, go to the same chair and do the practice for another five minutes. If you feel a positive difference, the next challenge is to increase the time to thirty minutes a day for twenty-one days. The next level of practitioner spends 10 % of the day in meditation. The expert level meditates four, eight or more hours daily.

Being attentive is the first feature of the *Platform* to create **Conscious Questions**. To increase *Attention* during our conversations, we can eliminate or reduce distractions, avoid *multitasking* and practice meditation regularly.

8. Connection

Connecting with another person is a primarily internal process that, done consciously, allows us to better understand the intellectual, emotional, axiological and spiritual side of the interlocutor. Thanks to the relevant information that we capture with refined *Attention*, it is possible to imagine predominant perspectives, emotions and values in the other that, in the first instance, will only be a hypothesis. After following all the features of the *Platform* iteratively, we will refine these interpretations better and better until they are a good reflection of the reality of the audience.

Once we have this understanding, real connection occurs when we are able to correlate the other person's situation and state with an experience of our own or others that we have previously connected with. This correlation is the best description I know of what empathy means to me. Personally, I understand empathy as the ability of a human being to connect with the intellectual, emotional, axiological and spiritual reality of themselves and other human beings. Another illustrative way of looking at this would be:

$$\text{Connection} = \int (\text{Comprehension} \wedge \text{Correlation})$$

Comprehension

To achieve a good understanding of the reality that our audience perceives, we can consider some practical aspects, both on an intellectual, emotional, axiological, and spiritual level.

Intellectual: Avoid assuming. The perspectives and points of view of others are best understood when they are built with their information and not ours. As a consultant, I often make the mistake of filling in information gaps with my own assumptions. This gives me speed in the process, but it causes me to make precision errors and, therefore, reduces my ability to connect with others. To confirm the validity of our understanding and/or gather more information, we need to demonstrate genuine interest to others through questions that have these objectives, as we will see in more detail in the *Demonstration* feature.

Emotional: Avoid judging. Emotions and feelings are what they are. They are neither good nor bad, they are information. *Fred Kofman, executive coach*, author of multiple books, including my favorite *Conscious Business*, in his *Conscious Business Coach*[12] certification program, presents emotions as signals that require attention to level a tension or cover an imbalance generated as a result of some event. The following table shows his proposed eight emotions, the typical event or story behind the emotion and what the action is to create the required balance, honor that feeling, or in his words, pay off the debt.

I feel sadness **Because I lost something** **And I need to mourn**	**I feel happiness** **Because I achieved something important to me** **And I need to celebrate**
I feel fear **Because something is at risk** **And I need to protect it**	**I feel enthusiasm** **Because something important could happen to me** **And I need to make it happen**
I feel angry **Because someone crossed a line** **And I need to make amends**	**I feel gratitude** **Because someone went beyond the call of duty** **And I need to thank**
I feel guilt **Because I crossed a line** **And I need to make amends and not incur**	**I feel pride** **Because I went beyond my duty** **And I need to give myself credit**

Figure 8: Table of emotions and the gap that needs to be covered

Since emotions are also information, it is necessary to validate and improve our understanding of them directly with the interlocutor, without judging them.

Axiological: Avoid debating. What is important and valuable to others is not necessarily important to you. Personal values are like the white lines on a football field, they determine the limits where the game takes place. Each person paints their own playing field, and it is not our role to debate whether it is well painted or not. Our role in creating **Conscious Questions** is to recognize and understand the field of values where our counterpart plays, so that we can connect, even if we do not agree or share it. Just like intellectually and emotionally, it is also important to validate and improve our understanding of the other person's values, without debating.

Spiritual: Everything happens for the best. A saint from India wrote in one of his verses "Sweet is His Will." More colloquially, but equally wise, my grandmother often says "there is no evil that does not come for good." Connecting with another person spiritually means that we have a deep understanding that the things that happen are neither good nor bad. Whatever is happening to our interlocutor is happening, without exception, for the greater good. This understanding invariably leads us to enrich our conversation with questions about what further learning is behind what is happening, and how to use it as fuel rather than blocker.

Correlation

The definitive way to connect with another is to develop holistic empathy. That is, correlating the intellectual, emotional, axiological and spiritual reality with our own, or with the reality of another person with whom we have previously connected. Establishing a correlation is creating a bridge between realities. It is possible that we have not experienced an identical situation to the other person, or that we have not felt the same or with the same intensity, or that the other person's value system is different from ours, but we can invariably find similarities with our own experiences or from third parties, that allow us to create that bridge to finally feel comfortable expressing phrases like: "I can see where you are coming from and I have an idea of how you feel because I experienced something similar," or, "I can understand you, because an acquaintance had a situation close to yours".

To establish the correlation, we can ask ourselves questions like: "What similar situations have I experienced?" "How have I felt in those situations?" "What personal values were at stake?" "What were my main learnings?" "What similar situations do I remember from other people?" "How did they tell me, or did I perceive they felt?" "What values did they want to honor?" "What did they learn?".

The *Connection* with the other person occurs within us, first by understanding and then by correlating their reality with ours. Now, validating and strengthening that connection requires us to react and receive feedback from our interlocutor. This is what our last feature, the *Demonstration*, is all about.

9. Demonstration

Genuinely showing our audience that we are connected to them helps them feel valued and understood. Furthermore, it is the step that completes the virtuous cycle of our interaction, allowing us to validate and improve the perception we form of its reality. The validation and improvement that we achieve through the *Demonstration*, evolutionarily strengthens the *Platform* on which we create **Conscious Questions**. A refined *Demonstration* is achieved using mainly five techniques:

1. Positive body language

2. Verbal cues

3. Reflective listening

4. Avoid interrupting

5. Supplementary questions

These ways of demonstrating that we are attentive and/or connected may have a greater or lesser effect depending on the person's predominant learning and, therefore, communication channel, whether visual, auditory or kinesthetic. Although studies show that people learn and communicate through the combination of these three channels[13], there is always at least one that generates the greatest impact on us. As you become better at identifying your interlocutor's main channel of communication, you will be better able to calibrate which forms of demonstration to use, at what time and with what intensity. As we enhance these types of fine-grained skills, we can rely on the obvious rule of thumb: *Make intuitive, selective, reasonable and timely use of all forms of demonstration, as guided by the interlocutor's reactions.* Let us review each form of demonstration and consider some of its nuances.

Positive body language

We can practice positive body language, maintaining welcoming eye contact, using facial expressions appropriate to the conversation, and nodding moderately. Now, everything has a fair measure. A fixed, permanent and penetrating gaze can be intimidating, while preferring to look between the other's eyebrows, while allowing my gaze to flow with the conversation, can be more natural and welcoming. Letting our gaze flow with the conversation means that, for example, I look at my hands while making a representative gesture with them; or that, I look at the horizon while I pause to think. A constant smile when faced with a comment associated with a sad situation can show not only inattention, but a total disconnection, while accompanying the emotional tone of the conversation with our expressions can maximize the connection. Nodding all the time like the little dog that shakes its head (the one that some put as decoration on their cars), can look mechanical and, instead of showing interest, shows distraction; while nodding only at key moments helps us convey that we are present and focused. Positive body language is a way to demonstrate *Attention* and *Connection*, which tends to have a greater impact on those people whose main communication channel is visual.

Verbal cues

Using short verbal signals makes it easier for us to show *attention* to those interlocutors in whom the auditory communication channel predominates. These signals are usually expressions such as "uhm", "uh-huh", "I understand", "I follow you", "yes", "sure", "interesting", among others. They are short, spontaneous and do not constitute an interruption, since they flow in parallel to what the counterpart is saying.

Reflective listening

Reflective listening consists of summarizing, paraphrasing or repeating to others what we have heard. This gives us the opportunity to quickly validate if we are perceiving the message correctly, in addition to helping us demonstrate that we are paying, at least, a basic level of *Attention*. This type of *Demonstration* is usually useful with both visual, auditory and kinesthetic. As long as they can see our reaction, hear our summary and respond to it, we are activating all three channels.

Avoid interrupting

Interrupting is an art. Abrupt and constant interruptions can convey a lack of interest or even make the other person feel disrespected. If we eventually feel we have to, we can offer an explicit apology. On the other hand, there are certain verbal signals that invite the other to specify their idea, it is like asking to speak. In meetings, both in person and virtual, it is common for someone to raise their hand as a sign that they want to express themselves. However, in a one-on-one conversation, the gesture of raising your hand might be perceived as strange. Nonetheless, sometimes we have interlocutors who don't stop talking. Depending on the context, it is healthy to use an abrupt interruption with an apology, or ask to speak with verbal signals, or by raising your hand if this is the case in a meeting with multiple participants. In any scenario, it will always be best to avoid interrupting until you consider it strictly necessary. One way to illustrate interruption is to think of a casual conversation with someone close to us who we like to chat with. Think about that person for a moment and remember a recent conversation. Did they interrupt each other? How? How did you feel when they interrupted you? How did you interrupt? Despite the interruptions, how did the conversation flow? Surely, if there were many abrupt interruptions or the other person talked endlessly, perhaps he or she is not the person you like to chat with the most.

Supplementary questions

A supplementary or follow-up question basically serves to maintain continuity in the conversation. Demonstrating our interest and connection with follow-up questions serves four high-level purposes:

1. Investigate information to refine the objective of a **Conscious Question** (Clear *Objective in Preparation* feature)

2. Gather more details so that the question is deliberate and focused (Key Information in *Preparation feature*)

3. Confirm our interpretations of the person's reality (Platform *Demonstration feature*)

4. Provoke deep and actionable reflections (main objective of a **Conscious Question**).

The magic happens when our supplementary questions are, in turn, **Conscious Questions**. When we do this, we are using the most powerful form of *Demonstration*, as it generates an upward spiral of *Connection*. It is this conscious *Demonstration*, which generates an increasingly deeper *Connection*, that manifests our power to influence others, to make decisions, to act, to see, believe and try different things, so that they achieve extraordinary results.

Returning to our analogy with a factory, the ninth and final distinctive feature, *Demonstration*, is what serves as a channel for us to deliver our **Conscious Questions**. The better the delivery experience, the more likely our user is to make decisions, mobilize, and mobilize their organization.

To close this chapter, I would like to summarize the most relevant aspects of each of the features of the *framework* in Figure 9.

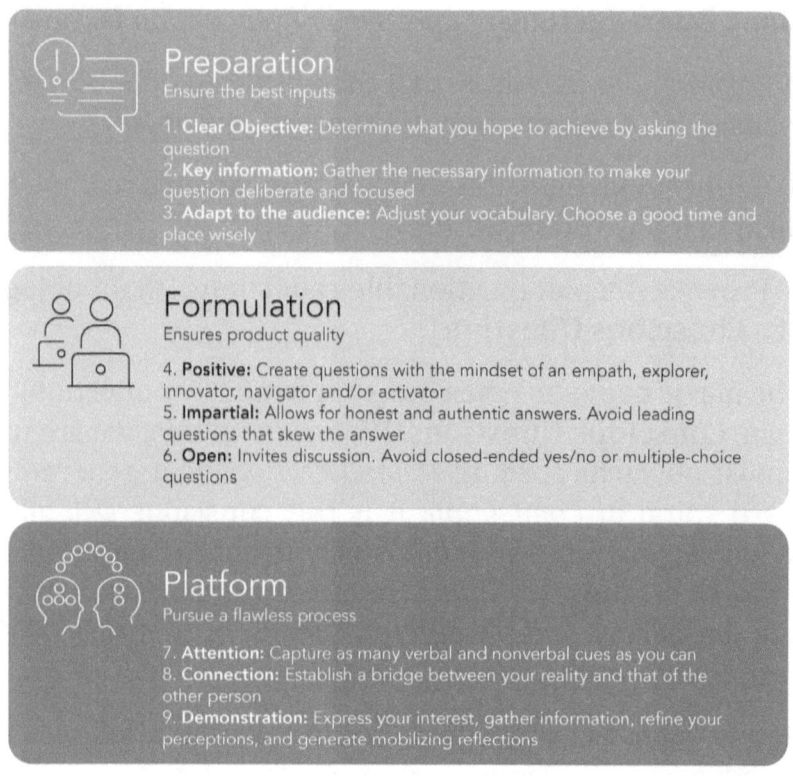

Figure 9: Summary of the framework to build Conscious Questions

As a prelude to Part II, where we will navigate everyday applications of this framework, I would like to propose a method for you to strengthen your ability to implement it. Now that you have used some of your valuable time reviewing the theory, it is time to complement that investment by learning to integrate the habit of **Conscious Questions** in any conversation into your daily life.

CHAPTER 4

Strengthening the Muscle

"Practice is the key to mastering any skill, but only if it is conscious and constant."

—*Michael Jordan*

How do you know if you have a well-developed muscle for asking **Conscious Questions**? The answer is, when ten or more people, in three or more different environments, tell you something like "[*read your name*] makes things happen." Although the answer is subjective, it has an objective basis. It is subjective because you will have to wait an indeterminate amount of time for others to start giving you feedback like this, based on their own perception of your performance. It is objective since they will tell you things like that, yes and only yes, in fact, those people have verified in real life that, thanks to your participation, even without fully understanding what you do differently, different results are achieved.

Conscious Questions

What motivates you to strengthen your ability to use **Conscious Questions** in your conversations? Think for a moment. If you don't have a clear reason to do so today, wait until you do before visiting this chapter again. If you already have a defined answer, then you have identified the engine that will give you the energy to rigorously and disciplined take on this challenge over the next three months. Shall we continue?

If we agree that asking **Conscious Questions** requires a special muscle (or refined skill), then we can think of a process to strengthen that muscle, similar to a training plan at the gym. Imagine that you are arriving at the gym with the motivation that you defined in the previous paragraph. That I am your coach, and I present to you a three-month plan that includes three types of exercises: Learn from your questions, develop the habit of preparing conversations and consciously evolve your *Platform*.

Now, before going into the details of each exercise, I invite you to act right now, reviewing your agenda and blocking three key slots, every week, for the next three months:

1. Set aside fifteen minutes a week and call it *I learn from my questions.*

2. Set aside fifteen minutes before the most important recurring meeting of the week and call it *Prepare for the next session.*

3. Set aside fifteen minutes weekly and call it *I Evolve My Conscious Questioning Platform.*

In the same way we dress for a physical workout, consider dressing with a notebook or digital space unique to this purpose. Avoid leaving your notes on any sheet or file, as you will end up wasting your valuable energy due to lack of rigor. Ready?

Just as a *coach would* do in the gym, I now want to present to you the recommendations on how to approach each exercise and with what tools.

Learn from your Questions

For the next three months, weekly, perform the following exercise for fifteen minutes. Think about a question you asked that impacted you during the week, either positively or negatively. Write it down. Now decode the question using a three-level rating scheme:

1. An **operational one**, where you will review the quality of the **Formulation**

2. A **tactical one** where you will explore the feature of **Preparation**

3. A **strategic one** where you will inquire about the **Platform**

Let's imagine the *framework* as an *iceberg*. The visible part is the *Formulation*, under the water we have the *Preparation*, deeper we find the *Platform*. Now evaluate what you see about the water, the final product, the question as such.

Write a question here for you to evaluate with the techniques suggested in this chapter:

_____

_____

_____

_____

_____

Operational assessment (Formulation)

Rate each of the *Formulation features from 1 to 10*. Don't spend a lot of time thinking about whether it is a 7 or an 8 (for example). Read the description and clarify what a value of 1 represents and what 10 represents and put in the first number that comes to mind. First you will probably have to go over the *framework* to remember which are the *Sages* or the *Saboteurs* in a positive question. This is normal and necessary, as you learn them by heart, you will master the definitions and begin to identify the mindset in your behaviors, and in that of others, on a daily basis.

How **positive** is the question?

1 - Denotes a mindset dominated by *Saboteurs* (perfectionist, pleaser, *hyper-achiever,* victim, hyperrational, hypervigilant, tireless, controller, avoider).

10 - Denotes a mindset dominated by *Sages* (empath, explorer, innovator, navigator, activator).

1	2	3	4	5	6	7	8	9	10

How **impartial** is the question?

1 - Very misleading, totally biases the answer.

10 - Very impartial, allows sincere and authentic answers.

1	2	3	4	5	6	7	8	9	10

How **open** is the question?

1 - Completely closed, induces yes/no or multiple-choice responses.

10 - Totally open, invites debate.

1	2	3	4	5	6	7	8	9	10

Tactical assessment (Preparation)

We have already assessed the most superficial part of the question. Now, let's investigate aspects that are underwater, the features of *Preparation*.

Does it have a **clear** objective?

1 - The intention of the question is totally vague.

10 - The question has a totally clear intention.

1	2	3	4	5	6	7	8	9	10

Does it consider enough **key information**?

1 - The question is totally accidental.

10 - The question is totally deliberate.

1	2	3	4	5	6	7	8	9	10

How **adapted** is it to the audience?

1 - Totally impertinent. The vocabulary, timing and place are totally inappropriate.

10 - Fully adapted. The vocabulary, timing and place are completely appropriate.

1	2	3	4	5	6	7	8	9	10

Strategic assessment (Platform)

Let's now move to the deepest and most powerful part of the framework, the *Platform*.

How refined is the **attention**?

1 - Totally precarious attention. Very limited capture of verbal and non-verbal cues.

10 - Highly sophisticated attention. Capture all available verbal and non-verbal cues.

1	2	3	4	5	6	7	8	9	10

How deep is the **connection**?

1 - Weak connection. There is no evidence of an intellectual, emotional, axiological or spiritual bridge with the interlocutor.

10 - Strong connection. The intellectual, emotional, axiological and spiritual bridge with the interlocutor is very evident.

1	2	3	4	5	6	7	8	9	10

How conscious is the **demonstration**?

1 - Totally unconscious. A fictitious expression of interest, it assumes perceptions as realities and lacks calls to action.

10- Totally conscious. Appropriate expression of interest gathers key information, refines perceptions and generates mobilizing reflections.

1	2	3	4	5	6	7	8	9	10

Sum all the scores and divide the result by nine to obtain the result that you can relate to a maturity level of the question.

Write in the right column, and in the corresponding row, the result you obtained.

Level	Result
Conscious (8, 10)	
Intermediate (6, 7.99)	
Traditional [1, 5.99)	

End the session by making two definitions for next week's focus:

1. What strong feature (rated 8 or 10) are you going to consciously use?

2. What weak feature (rated 5.99 or less) are you going to improve?

It is key that each week you prioritize a strong feature and a weak one to prepare your interactions. It has been shown that working on both strengths and opportunities can increase our performance, while focusing only on our opportunities can decrease it.

We already have a tool and a weekly plan so you can learn from your questions and continually improve them. Now, let's review the second part of the training that will give you an extra advantage over most of your colleagues. It is the habit of doing pre-work for your meetings.

Prepare your Interactions

For the next three months, weekly, prepare for the most important meeting of your week for fifteen minutes. You should create a list of three to five **Conscious Questions** that you can ask. As *Key Information*, consider the strong and weak features that you prioritized for the week (it is the result of the *Learn from your questions exercise*). To help you think about this list, I propose the following inspiring questions. By the way, I call these types of questions that inspire others *meta-questions*.

The following meta-questions are designed to address each of the *framework's distinctive features*:

1. What question would help you establish a clear objective that is aligned with the vision of the organization and the goals of your team?

2. Which question would allow you to gather key information and relevant data to make informed decisions in your executive role?

3. What question would guide you in adapting your message and approach to the needs and expectations of your audience?

4. Which question would help you stay positive and focused on opportunities for improvement rather than highlighting problems?

5. What question would allow situations and challenges to be addressed impartially, avoiding personal or group biases?

6. What question would encourage exploring possibilities and generating open-ended solutions rather than limiting predetermined answers?

7. What question would guide you to stay focused and attentive to the concerns, needs and ideas of your team members and other colleagues?

8. What question would allow you to establish an emotional and empathetic connection with your team members and other colleagues?

9. What question would help you demonstrate authenticity, transparency and commitment in your leadership role?

Your **Conscious Questions**:

1 _____

_____

2 _____

_____

3 _____

_____

4 _____

_____

5 _____

_____

As you may have experienced, *meta-questions* are useful in high uncertainty environments. In this case, I suggest using them, since the conversation where we will deploy the **Conscious Questions** is in the future, which implies too many aspects that we will not be able to control. It would be very challenging to establish the possible paths through which a conversation will flow. And even more so, create an exhaustive list of possible questions to ask with the interlocutor's alternative reactions. To better understand this, let's review the *framework* **Cynefin**[14] by Professor *Dave Snowden*.

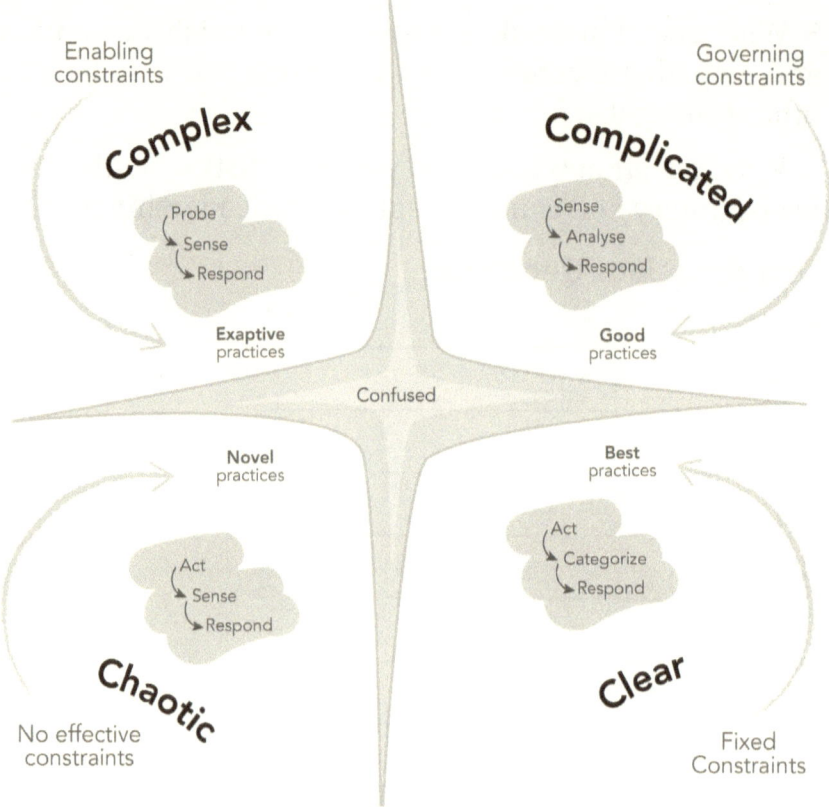

Figure 10: Cynefin Framework

A few years ago, I had a conversation[15] with Professor Snowden. At that moment we were struck by the idea of understanding how their framework could help an executive make better decisions. Similarly, this same framework can help us determine when to use **Conscious Questions** and when to rely on *meta-questions. Cynefin*, divides the universe into three types of systems (or situations):

1. Organized
2. Complexes
3. Chaotic

An **ordered system**, in turn, is divided into: clear and complicated. In a *clear subsystem*, cause and effect relationships are obvious, therefore uncertainty is minimal. Example, imagine that you buy a television, you take the remote control, and you see a button with a circle and a vertical line inside. You immediately press it and wait for the TV to turn on. Why? Because we have agreed on what that symbol means, and so much so that it is used by default on most electronic devices. The relationship of cause (pressing the button with circle and bar) and effect (turning the television on or off) is obvious, there is no uncertainty. In a *complicated subsystem*, cause and effect relationships exist, but they are not obvious. They often require expertise or analysis to be discovered. Imagine that the same television stops working. You pressed the power button, but nothing happens. The normal thing would be for you to review, first, aspects of the *clear subsystem*, that is, the most obvious cause and effect relationships, such as checking if the television is connected to the electrical supply. Once these obvious aspects, or good practices, do not have the expected effect, then we move on to mastering the *complicated subsystems*, and we will probably end up calling a television expert, whose expertise makes it easier for you to understand the situation and apply best practices for the solution.

To navigate an *ordered system*, closed questions are sufficient, since they allow us to navigate flows whose branches may have paths for Yes, for No, and/or multiple possible paths with certain conditions. For example, "Is the TV connected to the power supply?" Yes/No. "Which circuits should be checked first?" Circuit A, if X is happening; B, if Y happens in addition to X, otherwise check C first.

In a **complex system**, cause and effect relationships are not necessarily repeatable. Professor *Snowden* explains it this way: "Something will only happen in the same way twice by accident and not by design. The only way to understand a *complex system* is to interact with it. So, what we do is create multiple parallel experiments, to discover what is possible through practice and not through evaluation. This is a key difference: if the world is very complex, there are multiple factors that influence what happens and you cannot know in advance what is right. In a complex world we deal with the present, not the future. [...] In the complex field we try to encourage people—move them in small steps—towards a goal. It is difficult to navigate a complex system with good or best practices. This is the world of exaptive practices. When we navigate complexity, we start by using practices that worked for us before, knowing that we will fail, but we still use them as an experiment to quickly discover what exaptive practice works for us at that moment.

This universe describes complex human relationships very well. The question, which worked very well for us in one interaction, will work in a totally different way in another, and we will have to iteratively use the **Conscious Questions** *framework* to reach that set of questions that mobilize and inspire extraordinary results.

Finally, we have the system where *meta-questions make sense*, the domain of chaos. In the words of Professor *Snowden*: "In a chaotic environment, there is no relationship between cause and effect, everything is random. But if you deliberately enter this space, you can create innovation, or you can allow multiple opinions to form a future state that cannot be predicted. To navigate the chaos by establishing some possible future states and prepare some **Conscious Questions**, we can take advantage of *meta-questions*.

As your personal trainer, I have already suggested two exercises that you can easily put into practice if you choose to do so. The first will help you learn from your questions, as a retrospective, and the second will help you anticipate the future a little and be more proactive in preparing your interactions. The third and final exercise in this training plan is to refine your internal skills of *Attention, Connection* and *Demonstration*. While the first two exercises help you improve the "What" (inputs and products—questions—), this last one helps you improve the "How," to evolve your internal process to capture better inputs, process them more effectively and create better products. -questions-.

Consciously Evolve your *Platform*

To improve the *Attention, Connection* and *Demonstration* features that are part of the *Platform dimension*, we will deploy a simple, but powerful method to increase its conscious use. The following diagram contains the relevant aspects on which we are going to work.

Attention:

A. Reduce or eliminate distractors

B. Avoid the temptation of *multitasking*

C. Practice meditation

Connection:

D. Comprehension:

    a. Intellectual

    b. Emotional

    c. Axiological

    d. Spiritual

E. Correlation

Demonstration:

F. Positive body language

G. Verbal cues

H. Reflective listening

I. Avoid interrupting

J. Supplementary questions

During the fifteen minutes a week that you have in your agenda for this exercise, we are going to reinforce each of these aspects.

Week 1. Reduce distractors and eliminate multitasking

It seems like a simple activity, but it is not. List the main distractors you usually have during key sessions and kill them (at least for this week). Don't buy excuses. At first, you will feel that you are missing them, as if your brain was actively seeking the hormonal discharge derived from novelty or pressure situations[16]. When your body understands that you will no longer continue to contribute to that circuit of interruptions, then you will have that energy available to pay *attention* to more and more verbal and non-verbal details.

Do you have other communication channels that also distract you on your list of distractors? If you must attend to your chat while attending a meeting, there is surely something in your management that is worth checking. Likewise, if you must answer your boss's call when he calls you unexpectedly. If you answer your mom's call in the middle of a meeting, it's because you "want to" not because you "must". Commit, at least for this week, to eliminating *multitasking*.

I commit to eliminating the following distractions this week:

_____

_____

_____

Week 2: Meditate

As I told you in the previous chapter, I practice a meditation technique for executives called *Meditation on the Light or Meditation of the Science of Spirituality*. During the space of fifteen minutes this week, you must define the time and place where you will carry out this practice. It can be in a chair in your home, a space in your office or while you are traveling (if you are not the one driving the vehicle). Choose a time at the beginning and another at the end of your day. Since some people have night work schedules, it is best to define a time and not a specific time. This time could be, for example, before breakfast and before dinner, or after getting up and before going to bed.

Once the time comes, go to the place you chose, quiet your body, quiet your mind and focus. To achieve this, follow the instructions detailed in the article *How to develop our maximum potential.*[17]

I commit to meditate for the next seven days on:

_____,

right after:

_____,

and after:

_____

An example would be: I commit to meditating for the next seven days on <u>the gray couch in my room</u>, right after <u>I get up and take a shower</u>, and after I <u>take a shower before going to bed.</u>

Week 3: Focus on intellectual understanding

For this exercise, we are going to reduce the spectrum of intellectual understanding to the fact of avoiding assumptions, using some cognitive biases as inspirations for reflection. Before doing the activity, let's review the theory about what it means to have **high intellectual understanding**, what it means **to suppose**, and what **cognitive biases** are.

Based on the studies of psychologists *Charles Spearman* and *Howard Gardner*, having high intellectual understanding implies possessing advanced cognitive skills, including superior critical and analytical thinking, an exceptional ability to solve problems, learn quickly, and adapt to new situations. People with high intellectual understanding tend to excel in areas such as logical reasoning, creativity, memory, **attention**, and **information processing speed**.

According to *Daniel Kahneman* (Nobel Prize-winning psychologist and economist), "suppose" is a mental process by which a guess, statement, or h**ypothesis is made based on available information, although this information** may be incomplete or uncertain.

Additionally, the term "cognitive bias" was first coined by *Kahneman* in the 1970s. With his colleague *Amos Tversky*, they conducted groundbreaking research on cognitive biases and how they affect judgment and decision-making. Although they did not provide a single literal definition of "cognitive bias," their work laid the foundation for the current understanding of these phenomena. In general, a cognitive bias can be defined as a systematic tendency in thinking that can lead to errors in perception, judgment, or decision-making. Cognitive biases are the result of **mental shortcuts, known as heuristics, that our minds use to process information more efficiently**. Although these heuristics can be useful in certain situations, they can also lead to systematic errors when they are not appropriate or when applied inappropriately.

Now, let's put it all together. During a conversation we can be tempted to make assumptions, aided by mental shortcuts, and pressured by the speed with which we must process the information we capture live. To mitigate this, let's continue adding theoretical elements that will help us make better distinctions.

The act of "supposing" may be related to several cognitive biases. Some of them are:

- **Confirmation bias:** It is the tendency to search for, interpret and remember information in a way that confirms our previous beliefs or hypotheses. When we assume something, we might be predisposed to look for evidence that supports that assumption rather than considering contradictory information.

- **Anchoring effect:** This bias refers to the tendency to give more weight to the first information we receive about a topic and use it as a reference point to evaluate subsequent information. When we assume based on the first information we receive, we could be influenced by the anchoring effect.

- **Availability bias:** It is the tendency to overestimate the probability of events based on how easy it is to remember similar examples. If we assume something based on how easy it is for us to remember similar cases, we might be experiencing an availability bias.

- **Representativeness bias:** This bias refers to the tendency to judge the probability of an event based on how much it resembles other events that we consider typical or representative. When we assume something based on similarity to other cases that we consider representative, we might be experiencing representativeness bias.

During these fifteen minutes, reflect on a conversation you had where a supposition of yours caused you to ask something out of place. Remember what reaction your interlocutor or audience had and determine which cognitive bias(es) served as a shortcut but led you to a limited or counterproductive *Connection*. Finally, consider what you can do differently the next time you find yourself making similar supposition.

My supposition was:

_____

_____

_____

Based on that supposition, the question I asked was:

_____

_____

The reaction of my interlocutor/audience was:

_____

_____

The cognitive biases I used were:

_____

_____

_____

What can I do differently the next time I find myself making similar suppositions?

_____

_____

_____

A while ago a cousin invited me to his office. We hadn't chatted for many years, and it was a moment of reunion. We talked about his family, his four-year-old son, and his new pet. He told me that he had taken Tom to the office and showed me the hole he had made in the floor and in the desk. Then I asked him: "And why do you bring your dog to the office?" And he answered: «Tom. "Tomás is my son". I felt terrible, and from my cousin's expression, I made him feel worse. To be very honest, it seems like I erased the rest of the moment from my memory because I literally don't remember anything else. Representative bias told me that that type of damage was from a dog. I never imagined it was his little son who made them. Anchoring bias led me to assume that Tom was a pet, since earlier that week I had met a friend and his dog Tom.

This week, focus on identifying how many of your comments and questions come from suppositions and mental shortcuts. Dig deeper to minimize bias and better connect with the facts.

Week 4: Focus on emotional understanding

This week we will have a magnifying glass on our emotions. Start the countdown of these fifteen minutes remembering two meetings. One where "good vibes" predominated and another that was one of those typical "heavy" sessions. For each one, remember what your dominant emotion was and check if you created the balance that the emotion demands. A "good vibe" session is not just one where everyone seemed happy. That session may have been dominated by fear, but if you found ways to protect what was at risk, then the harmony of that balance contributes to maintaining the "good vibe." In the same way, a session where there is good news, there is joy, but the celebration and/or pertinent recognition is not carried out, can become "heavy".

Describe your dominant emotion in the session with "good vibes".

I felt _____,

Because _____
_____,

And I needed _____
_____.

A practical way to manage emotions to maintain the "good vibe" is to perform the action that each one of them demands. For example, your dominant emotion may have been anger. Since you took it as a sign and understood the gap you needed to close, you focused your energy on mending the boundary that another might have crossed. I know that it seems counterintuitive that a session where you felt anger is one of "good vibes." My promise is that the more conscious you make emotion management, the more you will increase your ability to make most of your interactions "good vibes," no matter what emotion you must manage.

Describe your dominant emotion in the "heavy" session.

I felt _____,

Because _____

_____,

And I needed _____

_____

Imagine that you felt gratitude, but you did not express it, you did not thank. That debt could alter the emotional state of those who went beyond their duties and make the meeting very "heavy." Since you cannot manage the emotions of others, always keep your focus and energy on how you feel, and how, by ensuring your balance, you can influence the emotional environment of the session and of others.

The rest of the week your task is to be aware of your emotional state. Whenever you detect an alteration, whether it is happiness or sadness, pause, do not react, do not respond. Write down how you feel, why you feel that way, and what you need to do to regain balance. If after writing it you think it's time to ask a Conscious Question about it, go ahead, otherwise find a better time or place.

Week 5: Focus on axiological understanding

What is behind the comments, decisions or behaviors of others? What is behind ours? This week we are going to focus on the second question: what values, what valuable things in the depth of our being led us to comment, decide, behave or ask something. For the next fifteen minutes we will review your personal values. First, take your notes and create five columns. Each column will contain a value. Then, go to my blog,[18] where you can find a list of one hundred values. Write the first five values in the list, one value in each column. Keep reading the list of values, one by one. Each time you find a value that you resonate with most, you must choose which one to change it to, crossing it out of the corresponding column, and adding the new one. At the end of the exercise, you will have a suggestion of the five personal values that, as you will see in the Helping Others chapter, demarcate the playing field from which you display your behaviors on a daily basis. It doesn't matter if these values are the ones that define your behaviors today or are the ones you would like to have from today. The key is the reflection that we will do during the week.

Value 1	Value 2	Value 3	Value 4	Value 5
Kindness	Loyalty	~~Honor~~	Freedom	~~Peace~~
		Discipline		~~Patience~~
				Love

Figure 11: Illustrative table to select the most relevant values

Make sure you have these five values visible during the meetings or interactions that you consider most relevant this week and read them every time you detect an intense peak in any of the signals from your emotional system, leveraging the muscle strengthened the previous week. In other words, whenever you are feeling intense sadness, fear, anger, guilt, happiness, excitement, gratitude, or pride, pause, look at your list of values, and give yourself a few moments to determine what to do next, fully honoring them. For example:

• Someone says or does something that makes you very angry. You detect the sign of anger, you pause and think, fully honoring your values, how would you react? What would you respond? When would you do it?

• You see someone you are physically attracted to and, even though they are not your partner, you feel intense enthusiasm. You stop and think, if you honor your values, what to do?

At the end of the week, you will have installed a very powerful circuit of conscious connection between your behaviors and your values. Naturally, you can take additional time to determine the values on which you want to build yourself in the coming years and repeat this exercise for as long as you consider necessary, until you feel that your reactions are in total harmony with what is truly valuable to you. At that time, you can focus your energy on other work.

Week 6: Focus on spiritual understanding

"Everything happens for the best", is this week's phrase. During these fifteen minutes you are going to remember two situations, one that happened five to ten years ago, and another more recent, from the last two to four weeks. These must be situations of adversity, conflict and/or injustice, a "bad" situation. Describe each situation in one sentence. For the first, remember what good things happened later, that, without that adverse situation, this blessing would not have come to your life. For the second situation, ask yourself: "What new possibilities and opportunities could come from this situation?" Write the first thing that comes to your mind.

Summary of something that happened five to ten years ago:

_____

_____

_____

What good things happened thanks to this first situation?

_____

_____

_____

Summary of a recent situation:

_____

_____

_____

What good things do you think could happen thanks to this second situation?

_____

_____

_____

To further practice this approach, during your interactions this week, actively scan for situations of adversity and ask your teams, "What do you think will be positive about this?"

Week 7: Strengthen the correlation

It is time to create bridges, correlating our reality with that of our audience through our own or third-party experiences. In the next fifteen minutes, think about two moments, one, where the conversation flowed smoothly, but powerfully. Typically, at the end of these types of sessions, people will express sincere gratitude to you and share what was truly a game changer for them. Normally, the bridge created will be very evident. Another, where the talk was somewhat unfortunate. Surely, you did not achieve anything mobilizing. You can feel the barrier and resistance instead of the bridge.

Recreate each moment and describe it. Look, like fast-forwarding and rewinding a video, to see where the correlation strengthened or weakened. Reflect on what went well and how you can continue to use it consciously. Likewise, learn about how the gap was created and how you can handle it differently going forward.

One conversation where I created a good correlation was:

_____

_____

_____

I consolidated the correlation when:

_____

_____

_____

Going forward, I will consciously use the following elements of success:

_____

_____

_____

A good example of a weak correlation was when:

_____

_____

_____

I weakened the correlation when:

_____

_____

_____

From now on, instead of A, I will try doing B:

_____

_____

_____

Imagine that you are in front of another person and a cube is in the middle of both of you. Your side is blue, but the other person's side is green, and neither of you can see the other's side. Since your reality is blue, a weak correlation means that you interact as if the other's reality is also blue. A strong correlation, or establishing a good bridge, means that even though your reality is blue, you can understand that, at the same time, the other's reality could be different. Thus, you interact seeking to understand what color the other sees to correlate it with experiences where you or other people also saw that color.

From this exercise, focus your energy for the rest of the week on identifying whether, in your key interactions, you are only seeing the blue side, or whether you are able to establish the correlation with the green side.

Week 8: Use positive body language

During the fifteen minutes of practice This week, you are going to start a video call where only you will be. While you watch your camera, you are going to repeat a list of three to five questions or comments that you typically ask, mechanically, without thinking much about how you are doing it, with the goal of coming out as close to how you act in your day to day. As you do this, notice how welcoming your eye contact is and how consistent your expressions are with the message you are conveying.

List of typical questions and comments to practice:

_____

_____

_____

_____

_____

_____

_____

As an alternative exercise, you can ask a trusted colleague or your partner to be your interlocutor. Propose a casual conversation for ten minutes but tell him what things he should observe in you so that in the final five minutes he can tell you about his reading.

Write below the main findings and calls to action to practice during the week:

_____

_____

_____

_____

_____

For the rest of the week, deploy the calls to action you considered above. An alternative to doing this is that, in all the virtual sessions you have, focus mainly on your camera. Pay attention all the time to your facial expressions, placement of your hands, way of sitting. This observation will give you better elements when doing an in-person display, where you will not have the camera showing you your live performance.

Week 9: Use verbal cues

Let's start this practice by listing the typical signals you use. Next, list the signs you admire in others. Both exercises are difficult, because normally we do not pay attention to these things. To help you with the first list, you can ask colleagues and/or people close to you about your typical signs. For the second list, you can first think about those people with whom you like to talk the most, and with them in mind, identify their common verbal signals more easily.

My most common verbal cues are:

_____

_____

_____

_____

The verbal cues I most admire in others are:

_____

_____

_____

_____

Reflect on the previous two lists and create a third list with signals that you want to use consciously during the week. Rest assured, this final list will have a mix of your current common cues and the ones you like best from other people. The most important thing is that you can have this new list close to you during the week, so that you can see it and use it with intention, while you automate it again.

I am going to use the following list of verbal cues:

_____

_____

_____

_____

It is important that you pay attention to how your audience reacts, so that you can refine your signals according to how they harmonize with people's reactions.

Week 10: Use reflective listening

These fifteen minutes you will make a list of transition phrases that will lead you to summarize, paraphrase or repeat what you are hearing. An example of these phrases could be: «Let me validate if I understood correctly. What I heard is […]" "I would like to paraphrase what I heard to see if we are on the same page" "I am going to share what I understood to see if I am following you properly." Then create a list of three to five phrases, very much your own. Include the ones you already use and take the opportunity to refine them.

List of transition phrases to reflective listening:

_____

_____

_____

_____

_____

_____

_____

_____

_____

During the week, your homework is to have these transitional phrases on hand to serve as a reminder to do these mid-course checks during a conversation, helping you intentionally showcase your reflective listening skills.

As you progress with the exercise, you will notice two things. First, each time your summary, paraphrasing or repetition will be more and more accurate. Second, when they are not, you will have more and better key information to prepare your next question.

Week 11: Master the art of interrupting

This will be a week of extremes. During these fifteen minutes you are going to list the spaces where, safely, you can display three ways of interrupting: abruptly, not interrupting and doing it in an artistic way.

Spaces where I am consciously going to interrupt abruptly (with apology):

_____

_____

_____

Meetings where I am consciously not going to interrupt (or ask to speak):

_____

_____

_____

Sessions where I will consciously make artistic interruptions:

_____

_____

_____

Make sure that the spaces where you will only make abrupt interruptions are the safest. That is, at the end you can tell the participants that you are working on refining your ability to interrupt, and that you chose that space to use the strongest method. Ask them how they felt and use their feedback as input to create your own style of artistic interruptions.

It is also important that meetings where you are not going to interrupt at all do not require you to make important decisions or are not highly critical to unlocking and/or accelerating any initiative. Also, avoid one-on-one spaces, since it will seem you are not interested in the conversation. Again, share your intention with the audience and ask for feedback to refine your artistic style.

To practice artistic interruptions, choose brainstorming or problem-solving sessions, since they typically invite debate and facilitate the deployment of this skill.

My own style of artistic interruptions includes:

_____

_____

_____

_____

_____

The relevant thing about the style you develop is that it facilitates conversations, contributes to making them effective, and helps people feel comfortable with you and what is being obtained from the session.

Week 12: Ask consciously

This is your last week of the training program to strengthen your muscle of creating and using **Conscious Questions**. During these fifteen minutes put everything together. Write down what your main improvements have been during these three months and what results recognized by others have been generated.

My main improvements during these three months were:

_____

_____

_____

Other people recognized the following results, which are attributable to my leadership style refined with **Conscious Questions**:

_____

_____

_____

Finally, talk to your team and ask who wants to be your **Conscious Questions** apprentice. You will be his coach for the next three months. Your task this week will be to help that person organize their work plan so that they can begin executing it as soon as possible. There is no magic recipe to achieve mastery, other than rigorous and disciplined practice for the necessary time.

We have reached the end of **Part I**, where you learned the theoretical foundations of **Conscious Questions** and established a training plan that you can use for yourself and to multiply this skill in others. However, you may still have concerns about what these questions may look like in real life, how to use them, when, with whom, and how mobilizing they can be. That's why I created **Part II**, so you can find inspiration for your daily life.

PART II

CONSCIOUS QUESTIONS IN EVERYDAY LIFE

Now that we have the theoretical foundations, I invite you to raise your repository of questions that will serve as a shortcut in your daily interactions. Below, you will find five chapters where I tell you anecdotes that illustrate how using Conscious Questions made a notable difference in the results. In addition, you will have an illustrative list of typical questions for each topic, which will undoubtedly serve as inspiration when preparing conversations and strengthening your own muscle. You'll find how you can use them to help others, make decisions, navigate difficult conversations, ask a leader for guidance, and empower work teams. This is just a small sample of a virtually inexhaustible field of application.

CHAPTER 5

Helping others

"The greatest good you can do for another is not only sharing your wealth but also revealing his."

—**Benjamin Disraeli**

One Thursday, in the middle of the summer breeze, with spectacular sunshine, around four in the afternoon, I was on a video call receiving feedback on my work performance. I can remember in my mind, as if it were an episode of an old series in high definition, the moment when I was notified that I was underperforming. Until that moment I felt self-sufficient in my professional career, as I had managed to build an industry reputation with results to back it up. You can imagine my frustration when that self-sufficiency built by years of hard work and effective results was swept away in seconds, along with a clear message of "you need to seek help". All of that was knocking on the door in my work life.

It took me several days to assimilate the situation, and to be able to organize in my head what steps I wanted to take to continue moving forward. I was able to begin to see the light when I talked about what happened with other more experienced colleagues, and especially when I incorporated the magic phrase "how can you help me?" into my dialogue. At first, I felt like a scam. I found a very deep belief in me that made me feel weak if I asked others for assistance, and since I always wanted to appear strong and powerful, naturally I didn't. Once I confronted that limiting belief, I found that, in fact, the continuous improvement that I had promoted so much in my career had humility as a governing value.

Once I reconciled my ego with the opportunity to learn and improve, I began to see more clearly the great power of the questions my colleagues were asking me. One of them asked me: "What have been the main lessons you learned from this situation?" Another said to me, "What will you do differently next time?" One more I remember was: "When you look back on this in five years, what would make you proud of yourself, regardless of the outcome of the assessment?" These and other **Conscious Questions** influenced me to do a deep review of my personal values, how these were connected to the values of the company where I worked, what behaviors I should maintain, which ones I should completely eliminate, and which ones I urgently needed to improve.

Today, in addition to being more open to asking for help, I have the personal commitment to find space in my agenda when someone seeks me out with the same intention. I maintain the hope that my questions can inspire that person, as much as they inspired me when they were asked to me. Now, equipping myself with a set of **Conscious Questions** enhanced my ability to help others, be they co-workers, friends, or family, and even myself. There are two sets of questions that I have found especially powerful and that I would like us to explore together: **Reinforce values and Build behaviors.**

Reinforcing Values

Personally, I understand values as a set of deep beliefs that frame behaviors. I like to see them as an iceberg. Above the water you see the behaviors and below the surface are, among other things, the values. These convictions are there, whether we are aware of them or not. That is why I consider it so important to provide ourselves with a set of **Conscious Questions** that, in a generic way, but applicable in multiple scenarios, allow us to influence colleagues, friends or family.

Since my son Matías was born, I began to reinforce four values on which he can build his own when he decides to do so. When we bathe, before going to sleep, when we get up, and in different day-to-day interactions, we repeat them like a mantra: "I am powerful, loving, intelligent, and wise." When we are doing physical exercise together, and he suddenly wants to stop a routine because he is tired, I like to say to him: "Son, you are powerful, remember? How do you think your power will help you get to the end? When he gets angry because he wants to do something and it's not the time, I usually comment: "Mati, it's okay to get angry and frustrated. How would you feel if you quickly reconnected with how loving you are? When he feels that he cannot master a task quickly, I am inclined to ask him: "Son, do you remember what makes you so intelligent? [...], exactly, learn from your mistakes and keep trying." When he wants to skip meditation from his bedtime routine, I mention: «Do you remember what is the source of all your power, love and intelligence? [...], that's right my love, it is wisdom, that unlimited supreme energy that comes from God."

All of these questions are possible because the values are not only known but are common ground for those involved. In the work environment this is more challenging for two main reasons:

1. It is rare to find someone who is clear about their values, to the point that they can list and define them with complete fluency.

2. It is even less common for people who have very clear values to disclose them openly.

These environments where values are unknown pose an additional challenge, as the questions require an angle, not only reflective, but also exploratory.

Several years ago, I was leading a team. A new member arrived, and we began a new stage of *forming, storming, norming* and *performing*[19]. The first storm came when, for the third time in a row, this colleague failed to fulfill a work commitment. I asked him for space to understand how I could best help him. For confidentiality, I'm going to call him *Andrés*.

—Hello, Andrés, how are you?

—Very good, and you Neo?

-Glad! Andrés, I want to tell you that I am happy with your arrival to the team. You are helping me evolve our approach, accelerating the creation of new capabilities. Tell me, what else do you think we can do to become a better team?

—[...]

-I love it. In the following workspace with the entire team, let's return to these suggestions and together define those responsible, dates and priorities. I also want to tell you that there is a specific issue that has been bothering me in recent days, and I would like to better understand and align expectations.

I'm going to tell you about three recent situations and you tell me what you find in common in all of them, does that sound familiar to you?

—Yes, of course, Neo. Anything to improve is welcome.

—The first moment was when we structured the first campaign. Second, when we review the presentation for sponsors. And in the third, when we specify the main messages for the workshop on financial management. Do you remember them?

—Yes, perfectly, they happened a few days ago. About your question, I'm not so sure what they have in common, but let me try. Maybe they are issues related to sponsors, but it would only apply to the last two. It occurs to me that it is something in my way of making presentations, since all three have a built-in document. But I don't know, Neo, could you tell me what's on your mind, please?

—Yes, obviously, the idea is to build. Exactly what worries me is related to fulfilling the agreed commitments. In all three situations we talk about a day and time of delivery or review. I felt that these commitments were not honored because these deliverables and reviews did not occur before the deadline we agreed upon. Now, I am aware that it is often not possible to reach certain results on certain dates due to multiple factors; However, if that were the case, you did not notify me of any impediment, you did not ask me for help, nor did you suggest a new deadline. But hey, this is just my interpretation of the facts, how much do you resonate with what I'm telling you?

—Neo, really, thank you very much for letting me know this. Regarding the campaign, I do remember the review we agreed on, but the truth is I still don't know how to do it. For the Committee, I was waiting for them to update me with information on the results before passing it on to you and to avoid you seeing something incomplete. And about the workshop, I honestly haven't had time to move forward.

—What you tell me seems very reasonable to me, and I appreciate that you are so sincere. Now, let's forget the facts as such for a moment. What do you think weakens me when you make a commitment and don't honor it?

—Trust, Neo. I think you trust me less; But what do I do if many of the things that happened do not depend directly on me?

—We totally agree. I feel that the value that is under discussion here is that of trust. A work team can reach high performance faster if there is an almost blind level of trust among its members[20]. Now, regarding your question, let's chat for a moment about what it means to me to honor a commitment, and see if we can build on that definition.

—Yes, of course, because for me, achieving a commitment is achieving the committed result no matter what happens.

-Good. Each challenge we face can entail a series of activities. These can be classified into three groups: under our control, under our influence, and outside our control. With this, we are all clear that, with things beyond our control, there is a risk of failing to fulfill commitments that we have acquired. How do you see that we can connect these levels of dependency with the three events that I used as a reference?

—You know, Neo, it's quite interesting to see it like this, since I totally depend on others to get the results out of the system. I can influence them to accelerate that delivery, but even so, it doesn't depend on me alone. In the campaign, since I do not have specialized knowledge, I was able to look for other experts or look for you to have more information; seeking more information was under my control. This is to illustrate some of the ideas that come to mind with your question.

—I think the conclusion you reached is fantastic. Well, Andrés, but there is another group of elements that you should consider before making a commitment. Before saying "yes," it's healthy to ask yourself: "How much does this have to do with my current goals?" "Do I need to check them first?" "Do I have the time required?" "Do I need to review and prioritize my to-do list before giving my word?" "Do I have the skills and knowledge?" "Do I need to learn something or ask for help from experts?" "Do I have enough resources?" "Do I need any tools or technology that I don't have right now?" The answers will give you negotiation elements. For example, about the campaign. At the same moment that you realized that you were not so clear, you were able to tell me that you could not commit yet until we reviewed it in detail. Or you could let me know some time before the deadline for the presentation to the Committee if I wanted you to send it to me without the final data, given the dependency. Or you could ask me for help exploring other ways to speed up information delivery. What do you think?

—It makes perfect sense to me. I will be more careful from now on, and if you see that I still need to improve on something, I appreciate you telling me and let's move on.

—Of course, Andrés, count on me, especially because I want trust to be an unbreakable aspect in our team, I really need to be able to trust you one hundred percent. Dates and deliverables are negotiable, but trust is not.

In addition to reinforcing values in the work and personal sphere, **Conscious Questions** are also useful with our friends. I like to meditate, I am part of a global, non-profit organization dedicated to transforming people's lives through meditation[21]. In this group I met one of my best friends, today. One day I called him to help me with an assignment that one of my therapists had given me. I had to ask six people in my close circle what they thought about my good and bad things; just like that, in black and white.

During the call, my friend was very generous about the good things he saw in me. When we moved on to the bad, among several, he commented: "You have a strong temperament, when the *Saiyan*[22] comes out, when you don't control yourself, you can become very hurtful." We ended the call without going deeper; However, his comment led me to question myself a lot: "Why do I lose control?", "Why do I allow myself to hurt my friends?", "What does this have to do with my values?", "What can I do?" do differently or better to control myself?", "What will make me feel proud of myself?"

This internal dialogue cleared the way for me. One of the six values that I defined for this life is **Unconditional Love**, and for me it means: *the energy that made us all and the material that makes us all up*. To love is to give the best of myself to others and to give myself the best of creation. Clearly, I wasn't giving my friends the best of me, in fact, his comment sounded like, in those *berserk moments*[23], he felt like he was getting the worst of me. I could find an infinite number of reasons to unleash my fury, such as: "He started speaking badly to me", "we have already talked about the same thing, at least three times or more", "it made me feel bad again", "he is always late", "it only causes problems", etc. In other words, I was conditioning the way I behaved to my expectations and standards, and in that disastrous game, I deteriorated my integrity and disconnected from my values, exhibiting Conditional Hate, instead of Unconditional Love.

Now, let's review an illustrative set of questions you can consider whether you're helping someone on your team, your leader, your best friend, your daughter, or your mom.

1. What is most valuable to you, regardless of the outcome?

2. What are the most important values to you and why?

3. How aligned are your actions with your values and why?

4. With your values in mind, what do you think could be different next time?

5. How much do you feel you are honoring your values in this situation and why?

6. How do your values guide the decisions you make?

7. How could you use your values to set future goals?

Now, what other questions do you usually use when talking about values?

_____

_____

_____

_____

_____

_____

_____

You can also share in the following link or QR.

https://www.linkedin.com/posts/neo-bernal_agiletransformation-agile-agilecoach-activity-7070759308866506752-aDzB

Building Behaviors

Now let's move to the top of the iceberg, behaviors. I have always been struck by how dog trainers are able to train dogs to perform incredible shows. In fact, there is a competitive modality where a handler directs a dog over a series of obstacles, which he has to clear in a clean and as accurate manner as possible, competing against the clock. This sport is known as *agility*.

Some trainers have stated that one of the techniques to train them is to give them a reward every time they properly perform the stunt required by the guide. The reward reinforces the message in the animal that, by doing more of what it just did, it is possible to receive similar rewards again. This increases the possibility that in the future, when the same stunt is required by the guide, it can be performed appropriately.

A few years ago, I accompanied a senior executive who used to be very good, but extremely good, at finding opportunities for improvement in everything his teams presented to him. In more direct words, he always saw everything bad, or as my grandmother would say, "he always lacks the penny for the peso." When I began to accompany him in his leadership style transition, we had the following conversation. For confidentiality I'm going to call him *Adrián*.

—Adrián, I have seen you interact with your teams in different spaces. Because of the closeness I have with several of them, in the hallways they tell me about the wear and tear they feel when they have work sessions with you. From your comments, they interpret that you like nothing, that it is never enough, that you are always in debt. In fact, this has begun to deteriorate professional confidence in several of them. They openly told me that they believed they were not the right people for their role. Has anyone let you know anything related to this?

—The person I consider my right-hand man has told me something, but not because he feels that way, but because of comments from others. Directly, no one affected has told me.

—Well, in these corporate environments it is usually a challenge for people to sit down with their superior and say something like that. But don't get me wrong, this doesn't mean they shouldn't look for you and talk to you directly, instead of poisoning the atmosphere by talking to third parties.

—Yes, okay, although now that you make me think about this, I'm not so sure that I have been open to people giving me feedback, even on my leadership style.

Conscious Questions

—Well, that is a very powerful reflection, and it can lead you to a very clear and punctual action. In addition to this, I propose that we explore possible reasons why your collaborators might feel minimized towards you. May I ask you some questions that may be uncomfortable?

—Sure, Neo, if there's something I don't want to answer, I'll tell you openly.

-Very good. In short, your colleagues mention that it is difficult to please you. How about we think about a case outside of work. Tell me, how would you feel if most of the time your wife only highlighted *"Always a day late and a dollar short"*?

—Neo, I would feel and have felt total frustration. And I answer you like this because what you are asking me was true at one point in our relationship.

—I see, do you want us to talk a little more about that?

—Of course, yes, besides, I think I can anticipate a little where you are going with your question.

—Well, tell me what you're anticipating.

—Look, Neo, before telling you about the work side, since we are talking about the personal topic, I want to share with you what I learned from the process with my wife. We just got married, she used to be very attentive to me, above all, she liked to take care of details that I loved. I was fascinated by telling her about situations with my friends or even at work, it was always refreshing to chat with her. Over time, her details began to disappear, and I also began to avoid some topics with her because I only received criticism. Since infidelity and divorce were not an option for us by mutual agreement before getting married, we sought professional help and began couples' therapy.

—I find this super interesting, thank you very much for sharing this story with me. I sense that in the future it will be very useful to help others, would you allow me to use it within a framework of confidentiality?

—Of course, Neo, don't worry. I will continue with the story. The therapy I'm telling you about has been a very beautiful process. And I say this because we are still going. It is for us like a continuous process of self-discovery that we find super refreshing. Furthermore, we believe that it is a great example for our children. I discovered that my wife had stopped paying attention to the details that I liked because she thought I had stopped liking them. And I got used to it and stopped telling him how wonderful they made me feel. I also understood that I had criticized her so much that she adopted that same way of reacting on certain occasions. Now, Neo, it seems that this issue of criticizing and ignoring what I like is an issue that I am consciously working on at home, but that unconsciously remains alive in my work.

—I think it is a very valuable find, Adrián. Leveraging the learning from your therapy, what do you think you can do differently in your next meeting?

—[...]

One day, reflecting on this and similar cases, I thought: "Could I structure a set of questions that would help people create or strengthen a desired behavior?" This *meta-question* led me to the following questions:

1. What is the behavior you want to change or reinforce and why?

2. What do you consider to be the underlying motivations or reasons for this behavior?

3. What are the potential obstacles or challenges you may encounter as you evolve this behavior?

4. How do you think you can measure progress in developing this behavior?

5. How can you create a support system to help you develop this behavior?

6. How can you turn this behavior into a new habit?

7. How can you make this behavior rewarding for yourself?

Exploring the iceberg of values and behaviors is certainly fascinating, especially for those of us who love working with people. We now have a powerful set of **Conscious Questions** that we can use in virtually any setting and with any type of person. Where there is an individual, we will have an iceberg ready to be explored. And each exploration will be a unique space to help.

Exercise:

What are your personal values and why did you choose them? If you have a clear answer to this, I invite you to help someone close to you to experience the same clarity. He who learns the most is the one who teaches others. If the answer is still unclear, the challenge is to start answering this question right now by writing a list of three to seven values that you feel define you today, or that you want to be your guides going forward.

My values and why I chose them:

_____

_____

_____

We just reviewed how **Conscious Questions** give us additional power to help others, and ourselves, reinforce values and build behaviors. However, it is rare that on a daily basis we question such fundamental issues, even though daily life tests our field of values and confronts us with the need to make decisions about what to do and what not to do. In the next chapter, we will see how questions help us make decisions and become a fundamental ally to help others do so.

CHAPTER 6

Making Decisions

*"I can't change the direction of the wind,
but I can always adjust the sails to reach my destination."*

—Jimmy Dean

The decisions we make today demarcate the path on which we will take future actions. Each choice involves rejecting, or at least postponing, countless alternatives that we could have taken. Now, why do we choose A and not B, C, D or Z? *Kahneman* and *Tversky*, in his *Prospect theory*[24] suggests that people make decisions based on maximizing the value they expect to obtain from an action based on the probabilities and associated rewards. On the other hand, *Kable* and *Glimcher*, found brain areas and neurotransmitter systems involved in evaluating the rewards and costs associated with options[25]. Furthermore, *Schultz* showed that the dopamine system plays a crucial role in evaluating the usefulness of options and in motivating decision-making[26]. Finally, *Jürgen Klaric*, an expert in neuroscience applied to business, brings together the results of the previous studies and communicates them in a simplified and easily memorable way. It says that we make decisions to **feel pleasure, avoid pain or save energy**.

I invite you to remember a relevant decision you have recently made; do you already have it in mind? I would like you to reflect for a moment on the following question: How much did these reasons influence the decision you made?

When we make decisions, we choose paths that determine the course of our lives. Consider these everyday scenarios for a moment: You get out of bed or continue sleeping (on your first day at work). You cross the street or wait for the signal for the pedestrian crossing. You get married or you stay single. Whether you have children or not. You read a book or watch a series. You take a job or start a business. You call your mom to say "I love you" or you watch one more story on Instagram. You brush your teeth today or leave it for the weekend.

Every day at work we also make decisions that can change the course of our careers; for example: attending an appointment with clients, taking or making a certain call, leaving a meeting on time, investing in a novel idea, hiring or firing someone, giving or asking for feedback, recognizing a great performance or result, challenging unwanted behavior, reacting aggressively or assertively, and the list could go on endlessly.

What is the decision that has most marked your work life so far? Why?

_____

_____

_____

_____

_____

Your decisions could inspire others, I invite you to share them. Scan the QR code or through the link.

https://www.linkedin.com/posts/neo-bernal_agiletransformation-agile-agilecoach-activity-7070759308866506752-aDzB

I remember a series of decisions I made a while ago, these led to me being fired from a job. Someone on my team had been "marked" by my peers as a person who could be an obstacle to getting their performance bonuses, including mine. After sharing their concerns, my colleagues informed me that they would recommend to our boss that we let go of that person, even though I was still finding alternatives so that he could adapt and improve.

I spent several nights thinking about how to handle that situation. I explored three options of action in my mind:

1. Talk to my colleagues so that they reconsider that position and delay their request.

2. Talk to my boss so that he would listen to my version before taking into account that of my colleagues.

3. Dialogue with the person on my team to inform them of the situation and accelerate the path of improvement that would allow them to stay in the organization.

After asking myself many times, "what is best for everyone?", I decided to do all three. I started by talking to the person on my team, she had been working in the organization for many years and, to my surprise, she took my message as a threat instead of a helping hand. The next day the situation became the hallway conversation of the entire area. My colleagues finally covered up with lies and a couple of days later my boss summoned me to his office to ask me to sign the resignation letter. That moment and the days that followed were devastating for me, I couldn't believe what was happening. During the process, I naturally did what I preached, learning from the situation.

Less than a year after what happened, I was able to find the great blessing behind that situation and confirm once again that everything happens for the best, and furthermore, that every decision has a consequence. Even though being fired initially seemed like a negative thing, I always maintained the connection to the unconditionally positive outcome. Before talking to the person on my team and after being fired, I asked myself, "Do I feel proud of myself, regardless of the (conditional) outcome?" In both moments the answer inside me was a resounding "yes."

Aware of the challenge that it would represent to present an exhaustive list of questions about possible situations for making decisions, I present below some questions that I have classified regarding certain daily events, such as choosing what to undertake, what to work on or what to study. These questions have been useful to me when accompanying team members, business unit leaders and organizational leaders, since, at the end of the day, it is not only business decisions that affect the performance of people and their work results, but also their decisions on a personal level.

I remember a one-on-one session with someone on my team. We were chatting about personal goals, and at one point I asked her: "What things, besides financial income, does this job bring you?" ». To which he replied: «It only helps me to meet new friends. I'm sorry to say it, but my desire is not to be a great software developer. "I really want to be an airplane pilot, but I saw that I could earn good money very quickly as a developer, to pay for what I really want to study." This question, which is more related to the personal level, helped me understand why that person was having challenges in their performance. She didn't really enjoy his job at all, since she did it only for money.

Choosing which Idea to Pursue

A lot of people within my circle consider me a natural entrepreneur. It must be because I started entrepreneurship at a very young age, motivated mainly because I wanted to give my family a better lifestyle. I saw my mother working at home all day, a great entrepreneur and my main mentor, and I didn't see my father at home, as he worked outside from dawn to dusk. However, I have to confess something, entrepreneurship is not an activity only for those who want to generate income as an independent or create a startup. In my corporate life I have also found entrepreneurial opportunities, especially because organizations are increasingly open to listening to new ideas from their collaborators. Furthermore, given the constant and accelerated changes in the environment, they understand that they need to maintain the spark of innovation to ensure the survival of their businesses.

One of the *Fintech* that I created was born from a Conscious Question that I asked myself: "Why are people with restrictions in the financial system limited to making online purchases in international stores?" After my first bankruptcy in 2001 I was left with unsustainable bank debt. This led me to lose my credit cards and with it, my possibilities of purchasing online in international e-commerce were limited. In response to my questioning, I found that payments in international electronic commerce, at that time, were based mainly on two methods: credit cards and electronic wallets (such as PayPal, Neteller or Moneybookers, today Skrill); wallets seemed to be part of the solution camp.

The search also led me to discover that more than 70% of Latin Americans did not have a credit card, a figure that decades later has not changed drastically in the region. I lived with the problem for many years, when in 2012, tired of these limitations, and armed with the understanding of "Why...?", I asked myself other **Conscious Questions**: " What can I do to pay easily online through electronics wallets? « If I am able to solve it for myself, how many people could need such a solution? ».

Once I resolved the situation for myself, I remember posting on an online forum that I could teach others how to ease the pain of paying online without a credit card. One person was willing to pay me for that advice, then another person, and then another. When I was able to verify that part of that 70% of people in the region were willing to pay for my solution, I asked myself: "How can I continue solving the problem on a massive scale without handing over the recipe?" The answer was a digital platform that became the most relevant electronic balance exchanger in the region at its time.

Large corporations also undertake. Several years ago, I accompanied an organization that asked itself the following question: "How can we enter a specific geography with a product that will lead us to be the leaders of that market in less than three years?" This led them to create a spin-off, an independent startup, that would create a new solution that changed the course of the market from its first year of operation.

I spoke with some executives who were asking themselves: "What is our next challenge in our continuous process of organizational evolution?" This led to a diagnosis in which I found that, among several key actions, they had a great opportunity to digitize their internal processes end-to-end. Subsequently, they asked me: "Which processes should we start?", and in a succession of **Conscious Questions**, they decided to undertake the creation of several teams with specialized roles to transform the processes with the greatest opportunity to improve the experience of their clients and, at the same time, at the same time, with greater economic impact for the organization.

If we think about teams, we can also ask ourselves **Conscious Questions** to decide whether to undertake an idea and include it in our solution map for the following months or quarters, or even in our task *backlog for the next days or weeks*. I had a conversation with a business unit leader and one of his leaders. The team was newly created and had the mission of transforming the customer experience during the purchasing process. After several ideation sessions, they had a long list of solution features. However, as in any *Design Thinking process*[27], after diverging, we must converge, for which, among other issues, we ask ourselves: «What are the main tasks to be carried out in such a way that we obtain the best experience for the client? ASAP?". The prioritized list included actions for the long, medium and short term. One of the short-term tasks was to reduce a form that the client had to complete from seventy to seven fields. The idea included making this new form available in a self-management digital solution; However, in said conversation, I asked them:

—How do we harvest those seventy fields today?

—Manually on physical paper —they responded.

—What is the minimum functional thing we can do for next week?

—Validate with the lawyers if the seven fields are within the legal margin.

—Do you see it functional? What if, in addition to legal validation, we validate the main hypotheses with five or ten clients in one of the branches?

—It sounds incredible, we would only need the legal team to give us a response in two days and at the same time manage with the branch —they answered excitedly.

—Who from the Legal department can we speak with now to get their support?

—[...]

—And about Branches?

—[...]

A week later, the team was sharing the learnings from their decision to undertake an experiment that allowed them to validate the main hypotheses of their idea.

Depending on the context, some of these approaches, or the spirit of them, can help you inspire the execution of ideas that could generate extraordinary results for individuals, teams, and organizations.

1. What is my main motivator to start/continue/scale this idea?

2. Why do I want to start/continue/escalate this idea?

3. Is the mission implicit in this idea aligned with my personal values?

4. Can I help others or the environment through this idea?

5. Would I be willing to invest all my money in this idea?

6. How can I divide this idea into hypotheses that can be validated in a few hours or a few days?

7. Would I feel proud of myself for participating in this initiative, even if in the end the expected results are not achieved?

How do you feel about this exploration of conscious decision-making questions? We have addressed some questions together so that you and other people in your circle can make better choices related to entrepreneurship. Just as you may be thinking, there are many other areas of life in which we face dilemmas, and for this reason I want to invite you to review the *framework* and the proposed exercises, so that you can continue refining your own **Conscious Questions**, increasingly adapted to the particular situation you are experiencing.

Choosing a Job

Most people with a full-time job dedicate an average of forty hours a week to said work[28], which corresponds to 33.33 % of our time from Monday to Friday. If we think about it carefully, choosing a job is relevant, since it involves dedicating at least a third of our week (not counting weekends) to activities other than our hobbies, family, friends or study.

As I have already mentioned, my life as an entrepreneur has brought me great successes and also great learnings. A few years ago, I was exploring my next step after my third financial bankruptcy. One day I received a call from a recruiter, commenting that they were looking for people like me to help the organization adapt better and faster to the increasingly voracious changes in the market. Several months passed in the process, in which both parties seemed to move forward "just in case". When I realized it, I had five extraordinary opportunities on my plate, between jobs and entrepreneurship. I felt that the exploratory stage was over and it was time to make a decision. I used several tools that had helped me before, I talked to many people, and yet I still felt the emptiness of uncertainty. One day, while making a video about finding personal purpose through a *coaching tool* I developed inspired by the *ikigai diagram*[29], I was certain that this was the path that would finally help me converge. So, I sat down, reviewed my *ikigai* by asking myself **Conscious Questions**, like the ones I will present later, and finishing that reflection, I was very clear about what opportunity to prioritize.

Sometimes we might make decisions equivalent to a job within our job. That is, some occupations involve changes in challenge, project or team more frequently than usual, say every three, six or twelve months. Given organizational dynamics that are increasingly network-like[30], it would be very useful to have a set of basic but powerful questions that help us optimize the time and energy we dedicate to navigating these types of constant changes. Below is a set of illustrative, non-exhaustive, first-person questions that I have used on myself and others. I sincerely hope they are as powerful for you and your circle as they have been for me.

1. Is this work/project/team aligned with my personal purpose, with my *ikigai*?

2. Are the organization/job/project/team aligned with my most important personal values?

3. Will I feel proud of myself in this job/project/team?

4. Do I feel like I lose track of time and space (*flow state*[31]) when I perform tasks associated with this work/project?

5. How much do other people recognize that I am outstanding in tasks associated with this job/project?

6. With this work/project can I contribute to the well-being of other people or the environment?

7. Can I see opportunities for personal growth in addition to professional growth?

The question of personal purpose is especially profound. Over the years, I have found that most people have not yet done that reflection or are not so clear about the answer.

If you want to go deeper, in the following video you can find a series of **Conscious Questions**, designed to help you find your *ikigai*. Remember to leave comments to contribute to the process of those who will come after you.

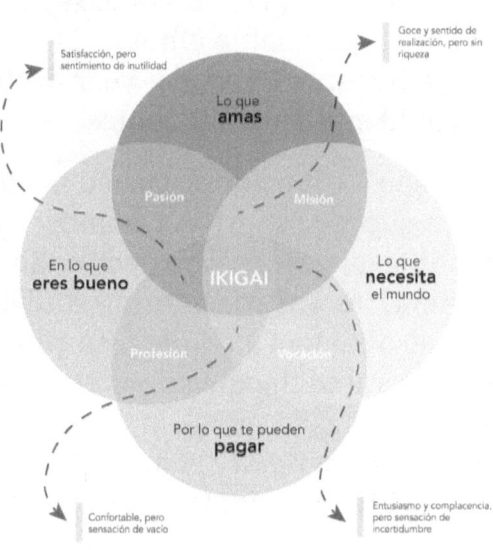

Figure 12: Map of purpose or Ikigai

https://www.youtube.com/watch?v=Pxp6RAfWYXI

Choosing What to Study

Thanks to the democratization of knowledge, boosted by the expansion of the Internet, computers and smartphones, it is increasingly realistic to consider a five-month training and aspire to a job opportunity with income equivalent to a more traditional five-year education. This is not to say that some trainings do not require a reasonable amount of time. Whether someone is making a five-month or five-year decision, the following questions could influence the choice.

A couple of years ago a friend approached me to talk about his career. He was a successful project manager and felt the market was demanding new skills for effective holistic project and team management. He was considering studying *Adaptive Management Tools*, also known as *Agile*[32]. During the conversation I asked him several of the questions that I write below, and thanks to the decisions he made, in a very short time he became the *Head* of *Business Agility* of an important European consulting company with operations in Latin America.

1. How proud will I feel of myself?

2. How long do I see myself doing this job?

3. What things, in addition to financial income, will this work or knowledge bring me?

4. What are the possible benefits for which I am considering this training?

5. How much well-being could you generate for others using this knowledge?

6. How motivated do I feel to put this knowledge at the service of others even if it does not represent financial compensation?

7. How much could this new knowledge help me grow as a person and professional?

Now, what led you to study what you know today? Or, what new skills are you considering developing and why?

_____

_____

_____

_____

Share in the following link what questions you asked yourself at the time or are asking yourself right now about your education.

https://www.linkedin.com/posts/neo-bernal_agiletransformation-agile-agilecoach-activity-7070797304189841408-lzel

Exercise:

Now I want to invite you to think about the question that marked a before and after in your academic or work life. If you could go back to those defining moments, what other questions would you have wanted to ask yourself?

What was the question that marked a before and after in my academic or work life and why?

_____
_____
_____
_____
_____
_____

What other questions would you have wanted to ask yourself at that moment?

_____

_____

_____

_____

_____

Choosing a venture, a job or a study are just small grains on the immense beach of decisions we must make in our lives. This, without mentioning that there are decisions that we cannot make alone, which introduces multiple points of view into the equation. The perfect scenario is that there are no differences or conflicts. However, it may not be as easy to agree in certain situations, which leaves us open to having some difficult conversations. Could Conscious Questions help us navigate them? Let's look at some ideas on how to achieve this in the next chapter.

CHAPTER 7

Navigating Difficult Conversations

"We are not thinking machines that feel, we are feeling machines that think."

—*António Damásio*

Difficult conversations are an inevitable part of life. At work, they can arise for various reasons: a disagreement with a colleague, the need to give constructive criticism, or the need to address a performance issue. Regardless of the situation, these conversations are often uncomfortable and emotionally charged.

Handling these situations effectively requires skill, empathy, and, most importantly, awareness. A powerful tool for navigating these turbulent waters is Conscious Questions. By using them, you can open space for understanding, relieve tensions, and create the possibility of resolution and growth. In this chapter, I will focus primarily on difficult conversations that stem from disagreement or conflict.

Some time ago, I moved out of town, and a friend kindly offered me his house while I looked for a place to settle. One Sunday afternoon, I arrived; he and his wife welcomed me warmly and showed me to my temporary lodging. That night at dinner, we inevitably ended up discussing my eating habits. Although I am vegan today, at that time, I was vegetarian, and my friend knew it. None of us had considered the possible implications of this on the household dynamics. I suggested that it wouldn't be a problem since I would mainly eat out, and if I did eat at home, I would handle the preparation myself. That's how we agreed.

A couple of days later, my friend invited me to stay for lunch together. Since I have known him, he has proven to be a great cook, and I did not hesitate to accept. Although I have never been fond of soups, out of courtesy, I ate the one he served me. It had a strange taste, but I thought it was due to my lack of habit at the time. That night, I felt very sick—my stomach was turning, and I had to vomit a couple of times. The next day, we crossed paths before leaving, and I told him how I felt, as I was still a bit uncomfortable. Surprisingly, he confessed that he had blended meat into the soup he had given me for lunch the day before and apologized, thinking it might have caused my digestive discomfort.

I was very angry because I felt he had crossed a boundary I never imagined, especially since he knew all the reasons why I was vegetarian and how long I had been committed to it. While listening to him explain his prank, despite my anger, I managed to calm myself since I was a guest in his home and didn't want to create a negative atmosphere. In that moment, I replied:

—Rolan, what made you think it was a good idea to give me meat?

—Neo, I'm really sorry.

—Don't worry, Rolan, I genuinely want to understand your reasons, because being my friend, your reasons are as valuable and respectable to me as my decision not to eat animal protein.

— Friend, the truth is, I'm worried about your health. You know I have been a high-performance athlete all my life, and animal meat is a fundamental part of a healthy diet. I don't want you to become malnourished or develop irreversible illnesses.

—I understand, Rolan, I can now see that your valid concern motivated you to give me meat, and I sincerely appreciate your concern and proactivity regarding my health. Would you like to know why I am calm about my nutritional balance by eating a vegetarian diet?

—Yes, of course, Neo, The more I understand your position, the better I can support you.

-Marvelous. Tonight, when I return, shall we continue this conversation?

—[...]

This conflict, stemming from differences in perception, unmet needs, and a desire for control, could have landed me in the hospital or could have ended the friendship. However, we discovered a common purpose (my well-being), and in a constructive way, we were able to overcome it, resulting in a strengthened friendship and harmony in our coexistence.

To better navigate difficult conversations, let's establish a theoretical framework around conflict.

Conflicts

A conflict is a disagreement between two or more people. We may experience conflict with a partner, or there may be conflicts between countries. But why do they arise? According to psychologists and experts in human relations, the seven most common reasons for conflicts are: differences in perception, scarcity of resources, unmet needs, poor communication, desires for power, cultural identification, and unmet expectations. Let's briefly review each of them.

1. Perceptual differences: Individuals perceive the world and situations differently based on their past experiences, beliefs, and values. These differences can lead to misunderstandings and conflicts. This concept is well-documented in psychology and social sciences literature. Cognitive psychologist Ulric Neisser is known for his work on perception and how it shapes our understanding of the world.

2. Scarcity of resources: Conflict can arise when resources (such as time, money, space, etc.) are limited, leading to competition. This idea originates from social conflict theory, popularized by sociologist Karl Marx.

3. Unmet needs: People often have needs and desires that may conflict with those of others. This is especially challenging in intimate or work relationships. This idea traces back to Abraham Maslow's theory of human needs, which suggests that conflicts can arise when basic needs go unmet.

4. Poor communication: Deborah Tannen, an American author and linguistics professor at Georgetown University, suggests that a lack of effective communication skills is a common cause of conflict. This includes misunderstandings, incorrect assumptions, lack of active listening, and not clearly expressing needs and desires.

5. Desires for power: According to sociologist Max Weber, conflicts can arise when people feel their status or power is being threatened, or when there is disagreement over who should hold more power or control in a situation.

6. Cultural identification: Edward T. Hall, an anthropologist and expert in intercultural communication, has extensively explored how cultural differences can lead to conflict. Differences in culture, religion, ethnicity, gender identity, sexual orientation, and other factors can lead to conflict if not properly understood or respected.

7. Unmet expectations: This concept is common in psychology literature, including Attachment Theory by John Bowlby and Mary Ainsworth, which suggests that unmet expectations in relationships can cause conflict. People often have expectations about how others should behave or how situations should unfold. When these expectations go unmet, conflict can arise.

What has been the most difficult work conflict you have experienced, and why?

_____

_____

_____

_____

_____

_____

Share and learn from others in the following link.

https://www.linkedin.com/posts/neo-bernal_agile-agilecoach-coaching-activity-7070800096530976768-j7wC

Let's return briefly to the story of my friend Rolan and the meat soup. We both had perceptual differences: I viewed vegetarianism as my best dietary choice, while he saw it as a significant health risk from his perspective as an athlete. Additionally, he was concerned that I might not be meeting the basic human need for a balanced diet. Finally, with the best intentions, he felt empowered to decide that I should eat meat that day.

It is essential to remember that conflict itself, like emotions, is not inherently negative. Often, it can be an opportunity for growth, learning, and strengthening relationships if handled constructively. However, let's first explore some problematic approaches to conflict management.

Poor Ways of Handling Conflicts

There are several problematic ways to manage conflicts, which can end up aggravating the situation instead of resolving it. Here I present some of them:

1. Conflict Avoidance: Some people avoid conflict at all costs, believing that if they ignore it, it will disappear. However, unresolved problems can accumulate, leading to resentment or misunderstanding. As Daniel Dana points out in his book *Conflict Resolution*, avoidance can lead to a deterioration in relationships and lost opportunities for personal and organizational growth.

2. Aggression: Some resort to aggressive behavior—such as insults, intimidation, or physical violence—to "win" a conflict. This can be extremely damaging for all parties involved and, rather than resolving the conflict, can escalate it and cause further harm. According to Professor Robert Bacal in his book *The Complete Idiot's Guide to Dealing with Difficult Employees*, aggression can lead to psychological harm, a hostile work environment, and reduced productivity.

3. Passivity: Some people give in to a conflict to keep the peace, even when they disagree. This attitude can lead to a buildup of resentments and frustrations, ignoring important needs or problems. Dr. Thomas Gordon, in his book *Leadership Effectiveness Training*, mentions that passivity can lead to a lack of personal satisfaction and undervaluing oneself in a conflict.

4. Competition: A competitive or "win-lose" mentality can also be harmful. Here, one person focuses on winning at all costs without considering the needs or feelings of the other party. Dr. Kenneth Thomas and Ralph Kilmann, in their Thomas-Kilmann conflict management model, suggest that this approach can damage relationships and increase hostility.

5. Manipulative maneuvers: Some people try to manipulate others to get their way, using tactics such as blaming, victimization, deception, or emotional exploitation. According to George K. Simon in his book *In Sheep's Clothing: Understanding and Dealing with Manipulative People*, manipulative tactics can cause emotional damage, erode trust, and create a toxic environment.

Each of these strategies has negative consequences and can exacerbate a conflict rather than resolve it. Generally, it is important to approach conflicts in an open, honest, and respectful manner, considering the needs and feelings of all parties involved.

Constructive Ways to Manage Conflicts

According to Fred Kofman, the most effective way to manage conflict is through Constructive Collaboration, which occurs in five steps:

1. Find a common purpose.

2. Understand the essential needs of the parties involved.

3. Plan how to best meet these needs.

4. Commit to specific actions to implement the plan.

5. Follow up on commitments and resolve mid-course challenges.

Let's look at each in more detail:

1. Find a common purpose: This is the crucial first step because it establishes common ground between the conflicting parties. When people have a shared purpose or goal, they are more likely to work together to achieve it, despite their differences. Additionally, it provides a framework for conflict resolution—discussions and decisions can be oriented towards achieving this common purpose.

2. Understand the essential needs of the parties involved: Understanding each person's needs is essential to finding an acceptable solution for all parties. Sometimes conflicts arise simply from misunderstandings or a lack of communication. By taking the time to understand each person's needs and reasons, new ways to resolve conflict may emerge. By using the *Connection* muscles (developed in Chapter 4), we can gain a deeper understanding of intellectual, emotional, and value-based needs, better equipping us to address conflict.

3. Plan how to best meet these needs: Once everyone's needs are understood, the next step is to create a plan that addresses these needs as best as possible. This may require creativity and thinking outside the box, as solutions may need to satisfy multiple needs simultaneously. The time and effort invested in this stage often pay off in the long term.

4. Commit to specific actions to implement the plan: It is essential that all parties commit to specific actions to implement the plan. This commitment demonstrates that everyone is serious about resolving the conflict and willing to do their part. Additionally, specific commitments are easier to track and measure than vague or general promises.

5. Follow up on commitments and resolve mid-course challenges: Finally, once the plan has been implemented, it's important to follow up and ensure everyone follows through on their commitments. Additionally, unforeseen challenges or problems may arise, so it is important to be prepared to address these issues as they come up, including new conflicts or difficult conversations. This may require ongoing adaptation and adjustment but is crucial to the resolution process.

Several years ago, I presented a work plan for an organizational transformation process to the founder of an educational institution. This plan included a leadership focus involving the founder and acting CEO and his primary team, with an assessment of his leadership style. Everything was going smoothly until this point. Suddenly, the founder no longer agreed with the transformation plan. I asked a few questions to understand his disagreement, but his answers were vague and tinged with nervousness. I suggested we review the plan privately before rejoining the rest of his team, and he agreed.

—[...]

— By the way, Jorge, I noticed you seemed a bit nervous during the transformation plan presentation. Would you like to share what caused your disagreement?

— Neo, we need people here to be better organized and more productive. They waste time, and I often see them on social media. Why do you want to assess my leadership style? I am a recognized leader in Latin America, followed by millions of people. My leadership is not in question.

—Jorge, you're right—you are a great leader, and your position isn't under question. Furthermore, I agree with you that the goal of this effort is to make your institution more economically productive while continuing its mission to educate more people in Latin America through the internet. Are we on the same page so far?

— Yes, but I still don't see the point of the leadership assessment.

— Now that we know we share the same objective, I'd like to explain how the leadership aspect is connected and how it can accelerate productivity. [...]

After explaining it further and discussing his discomfort with the assessment, Jorge admitted that he felt exposed having the entire company comment on him. Why do you think Jorge felt this way? Ultimately, with additional agreements, Jorge agreed to move forward with the transformation plan, including the leadership module.

Consider these key questions to navigate a difficult conversation using constructive collaboration:

1. What is the real problem we want to solve?

2. How does this challenge make you feel?

3. How does my perspective make you feel?

4. What other strategies can we consider to achieve our purpose while balancing our expectations?

5. What commitments are necessary to implement this plan?

6. How do you feel about your commitments and mine?

7. How can we check progress regularly and solve mid-course issues?

Conscious Questions help us navigate difficult conversations when we intend to collaborate constructively. This collaboration, done impeccably, can undoubtedly lead to extraordinary results.

Exercise:

Reflect on your work environment. What conflicts have you been unable or unwilling to address constructively? Rank them, putting first the one that demands the most mental and emotional energy from you. Select the top three and establish an action plan to guide difficult conversations and ultimately manage these conflicts constructively.

The unresolved work conflicts are:

_____

_____

_____

_____

_____

_____

The three conflicts that drain my energy the most are:

_____

_____

_____

Follow two or three key steps for each conflict:

Conflict 1:
_____
_____
_____
_____
_____

Conflict 2:
_____
_____
_____
_____
_____

Conflict 3:
_____
_____
_____
_____
_____

We now have additional tools for navigating difficult conversations involving disagreements. But what if we fail to address the situation constructively, or if little or nothing improves despite a work plan? If so, it may be necessary to seek help from someone with more experience or authority. In the next chapter, we'll explore how to use **Conscious Questions** to ask a leader for guidance.

CHAPTER 8

Seeking Guidance from a Leader

*"What is most detrimental to our learning
It is our tendency to forget that we are free to ask for help."*

—*Carl Rogers*

We find leadership figures in all social structures. In families, our father may have one leadership role, and our mother another; both are leaders. Among friends, some lead the Friday outings, while others lead cooking gatherings. At work, we have leaders who simply wield authority—whom we often call bosses—as well as leaders who are genuinely interested in us and support our career growth. There are technical leaders and leaders in work methodologies, strategic leaders, and operational leaders. Since leadership has so many nuances, I want to suggest a common framework, my favorite on the subject.

In his book *Primal Leadership*[33], Daniel Goleman describes six leadership styles, each with its own set of characteristics and appropriate contexts for effective use:

1. Visionary: This leader mobilizes people toward a shared vision and is most effective when a new direction is needed. Their emotional clarity and enthusiasm are contagious. However, this style may be less effective when a more collaborative approach is needed or when people require more guidance and coaching.

2. Coach (or Developmental): This leader focuses on the personal development of team members, most effective when individuals need to improve their skills in the long term. However, it may be less effective when the team requires immediate results or when team members are not open to learning and change.

3. Conciliator: This leader creates harmony and builds strong emotional relationships. This style is most effective in times of stress, when healing conflicts, or when boosting team morale and cohesion. It can be less effective when a clear direction or rigorous team performance is needed.

4. Democratic: This leader encourages participation and collaboration, ideal when gathering ideas and securing the team's buy-in is necessary. However, this style may be less effective in crises that demand quick and decisive action.

5. Exemplifier (or Pacesetter): This leader sets high standards of performance and embodies these standards. This style can be effective for achieving quick results from a highly motivated and competent team but may be less effective if team members feel overwhelmed by demands or need more guidance and support.

6. Dominant (or Coercive): This leader demands immediate obedience and exercises control through authority. This style can be effective in crises or with problematic employees, but overuse can stifle the team's initiative and flexibility.

Goleman suggests that the most effective leaders are those who can shift fluidly between these leadership styles, adapting to the needs of their team and the demands of the situation. I personally refer to this model as Adaptive Leadership.

The clearest example of an adaptive leader I know is my mother. For as long as I can remember, she has expertly navigated all six aspects Goleman describes. She is highly democratic when it comes to designing Christmas decorations, ensuring everyone participates in the process—a family tradition we all look forward to each year. During the most challenging economic crisis our family faced, she took the helm, guiding us like a captain through a storm to an island of economic stability and abundance. And to this day, she remains dedicated to providing me with the educational foundation that has shaped my professional career.

Who is your primary adaptive leadership model and why?

_____
_____
_____
_____
_____
_____
_____
_____
_____
_____

Get inspired and inspire others by sharing your model.

https://www.linkedin.com/posts/
neo-bernal_agiletransformation-
agile-agilecoach-activity-
7070803282721435649-MG_O

A week after beginning the implementation of a large-scale organizational transformation, we were notified by the government that we had to stay home for health reasons. This crisis required a swift shift to a dominant style to keep the company afloat. I met with the CEO to ask for guidance. The organization's goals were typically reached by consensus among the Board, the CEO, and his core team. However, there was no time for that process. We agreed on an urgent call, and I asked him: "Francisco, what are the three metrics the organization should prioritize to navigate this uncertain time as autonomously as possible?" He looked at me, surprised by the direct question. After a few seconds, he listed them and set a health threshold for each. Months later, his organization's results were the best in its industry domestically and within its global business group. No one questioned, and the entire organization focused on prioritizing their efforts around those goals.

When facing a professional challenge, ask yourself which aspects of adaptive leadership it touches on. Is it an issue of lack of clarity on where you, the project, the team, or the organization are headed? Or perhaps it's related to an organizational crisis or a problematic team dynamic. Once you identify this connection, consider who you've seen successfully tackle similar challenges in the past. It could be your boss or someone in a different area or organization. Reach out to that model for guidance using Conscious Questions.

Here are three questions for each leadership style that can help address related challenges:

1. Visionary:

a. Could you help us better understand the overall vision and how our current work aligns with it?

b. What does success mean, and how does it relate to your vision for this project/team/organization?

c. How can we contribute to the vision, and what can we do if we encounter obstacles along the way?

2. Coach:

a. Could you provide more feedback on how I can improve in my current role?

b. What could be my next professional development goals, and what paths could I take to achieve them?

c. How can you support my skill development and prepare me for future leadership opportunities?

3. Conciliator:

a. How could we work together to improve team cohesion and morale?

b. If conflicts arise within the team, what approach will we take to resolve them?

c. Could we discuss ways to strengthen our working relationships and foster a more collaborative environment?

4. Democratic:

a. How could we create more opportunities for team members to contribute ideas and feedback?

b. How can we address disagreements or conflicts that arise during team discussions?

c. What mechanisms can we establish to ensure all voices are heard and valued?

5. Exemplary:

a. Could you clarify your expectations and how we can meet the high standards you have set?

b. How can we manage pressure if we feel overwhelmed by work demands?

c. Could you help us balance performance with personal well-being?

6. Dominant:

a. Could you provide more space for the team to take initiatives and make decisions?

b. If I feel my ideas or contributions are being stifled, how might I address this with you?

c. If results have been disappointing for a while, how can you help us get back on track with positive outcomes?

I was accompanying the CEO of an organization during his transition in leadership style, amidst a transformation of organizational structure and ways of working. In the first business unit where we were testing some of the transformation hypotheses, we encountered a team that had developed a digital solution to assist the sales force. However, adoption of the solution was very slow, and there was no improvement in business results attributable to the tool. Upon further investigation, I identified a dominant CEO stance that was holding the team back. The CEO had instructed the team to deliver the tool on tablets, as he believed that using cell phones with potential customers would deteriorate the experience and, consequently, reduce sales.

After learning this from the team, I scheduled a conversation with the CEO to encourage a shift towards his more visionary, democratic, and conciliatory styles, helping him reflect on whether his dominant stance was still necessary. To maintain confidentiality, I'll refer to him as Simón.

—Hello, Simon, how are you?

—Hello, Neo. I missed our meetings already.

—Yes, a week of vacation during an organizational transformation feels like an eternity.

-Totally agree.

—Simon, this week I was chatting with your sales team and the team developing the digital solution for them.

—Yes, I feel like we've invested a lot in that team, yet I still don't see results.

— I am glad you mentioned that. The lack of results also caught my attention. Has the team communicated any main blockers to you?

—No, Neo, not so far. I imagine the team leader, unit leader, or vice president is working on it. Do you think I need to know the details?

— When it comes to a strategic initiative, it's always beneficial for you to be closely involved. However, in this case, there's something directly related to you, and I'd like your help to understand how I can contribute to accelerating results.

— Of course, Neo. Tell me more.

— Do you have a specific stance regarding the device salespeople should use with the solution?

— Yes. They've suggested using cell phones for the sales force several times, but I can't picture them showing quotes on small screens. I think a tablet screen is more appropriate. I'd feel uncomfortable if someone showed me information on a cell phone.

— I see. So, from your personal experience, you feel the best solution is to deploy tablets rather than cell phones. Did I understand correctly?

— Yes, Neo. And I also feel that my potential clients would likely share my perspective.

— Understood. Do you think there might be a way to validate whether potential customers' experiences would genuinely deteriorate if they saw your product information on a cell phone versus a tablet? Just so data could support your position.

— Hmm, Neo, I'm concerned we may lose the investment in tablets at this stage.

— Well, I have good news. Out of your five hundred salespeople, only thirty currently have tablets, as the team encountered a purchasing issue.

— Phew! No wonder I haven't seen results, ha, ha, ha.

— Would you consider scaling the tool if, within a week, we verify that using cell phones does not deteriorate the prospect's experience or conversion rate?

— That sounds ideal. Of course, if we verify what you're saying, my opinion would be secondary, and the facts would speak for themselves. In fact, I have some ideas to make it work without purchasing more cell phones [...].

During the following week, the team prepared everything technologically so that an additional thirty salespeople could use the solution on their own or even on the client's cell phones, allowing the first group of thirty to serve as a control group. One week later, the results were overwhelming: The customer experience improved, as most preferred to follow the process on their own cell phones with the seller's assistance, and the conversion rate increased compared to the numbers achieved with tablets.

Exercise:

Reflect on a recent situation you resolved with the guidance of a leader. What prompted you to seek their help? What key lessons did you learn from the experience?

_____

_____

_____

_____

_____

Seeking guidance can accelerate the path to extraordinary results. Now, consider yourself in a leadership role within a team or organization. What if you aren't perceived as a model of leadership? Or, what if you are, but your team doesn't look to you for guidance? These questions encourage a proactive stance, which we will address in the next chapter. Let's explore the power of **Conscious Questions** in enhancing teamwork in day-to-day scenarios.

CHAPTER 9

Empowering Work Teams

"The question is not who is going to allow me; but who is going to stop me."

—*Ayn Rand*

To picture a high-performance team, let us think of sports. I grew up playing and watching soccer, so I will use that as my reference here. According to statistics, Real Madrid Football Club holds the most titles in the Champions League, a competition that brings together the best teams from various football federations around the world. Statistically, Real Madrid stands as one of the highest-performing teams in recent years. But what makes them so powerful? I will venture an opinion—not because I have studied Real Madrid but because I have coached teams and organizations that reached levels of performance they had not imagined.

Several years ago, I was invited to be the Performance Coach for a team responsible for creating a digital solution to help doctors and patients better manage medical history and consultation interactions. When I arrived, I found a demotivated team; their last strong result had been two years prior, and their supervisors only expressed complaints and grievances. I spent my first week holding one-on-one conversations with each team member and everyone involved in the initiative. In each conversation, I ensured a 360° view of the situation with questions such as:

1. Why do we do what we do? How do we know we are getting closer to our goal?

2. Who are the people involved in the project, and how are they organized?

3. What are the team's typical internal routines and interactions with stakeholders?

4. How do you feel? How do you think others involved in this initiative feel?

5. How proud are you of the technology and technical practices being used?

I grouped my findings into five areas: Strategy, Structure, Processes, People, and Technology. First, we refined the **Strategy** by defining a clear direction, establishing success metrics, and involving doctors and patients in developing the solution. In parallel, we made **Structure** adjustments, adding necessary roles and evolving those with limited value. We established rigorous synchronization Processes to enhance stakeholder engagement and continuous improvement through early and frequent feedback. Additionally, we enhanced the **Technology** to ensure daily feature-building capabilities and the possibility to pilot with end users on the same day.

These improvements had an immediate effect on results delivery; however, they were still marginal relative to our aspirations. The most essential and empowering dimension—the **People** dimension—still needed attention.

But how does one empower people? How does one mobilize their soul, emotions, mind, and body? One approach is by helping them find reasons to act—motivation. Daniel H. Pink, in his book *Drive: The Surprising Truth About What Motivates Us*, argues that traditional motivation methods based on external incentives like money or recognition (known as "Motivation 2.0") have become obsolete. In their place, Pink proposes "Motivation 3.0," built on three core elements: Purpose, Autonomy, and Mastery.

1. Purpose: Purpose is the need to do something meaningful beyond oneself. Leaders foster purpose by helping team members reflect on their personal purpose, understand the team's and organization's purpose, and connect the two. An exclusive focus on external profits and rewards can make people feel disconnected from their work, lacking a link between their inner motivation and daily tasks.

2. Mastery: Mastery is the drive to improve in something that matters. Leaders activate mastery by providing opportunities for continuous learning and personal development, encouraging challenges suited to each individual's skill level, and offering constructive feedback. Monotony, lack of challenge, and absence of feedback should be avoided, as these can make people feel stuck and unmotivated.

3. Autonomy: Pink defines autonomy as the need to control one's actions and decisions. Leaders activate autonomy by granting teams the freedom to decide how, when, and on what they work. Avoiding excessive control is key, as it can drain motivation and reduce creativity and engagement.

Pink's "Motivation 3.0" suggests that people are most motivated when they have a clear purpose, opportunities to develop expertise, and autonomy over their decisions. So, how do we translate this theory into practice?

People Dimension: While we worked on the other four dimensions, I held weekly sessions with each team member, using the Ikigai map (previously mentioned in this book) to help them reflect on their personal purpose. For some, a single session was enough; for others, it took three or more sessions to achieve clarity and resonance. Once the individual reflections were completed, I organized a workshop with the team and stakeholders to review the organization's purpose and create the team's purpose, which did not exist prior. I took responsibility for making these purposes visible and used them as a North Star, helping each person align their personal purpose with the team's and organization's purpose during one-on-one sessions. It did not work for everyone: out of ten team members, seven found good alignment, two could not clarify their personal purpose, and one struggled to align with the team's purpose.

Some inside and outside the team were skeptical about this dimension, often viewed as "fluffy." One supervisor commented, "Why all this talk? At the end of the day, I pay them to do their job." This perspective overlooked the fact that his leadership style had contributed to the team's lack of results for years.

I implemented practical applications for mastery and autonomy as well, creating a continuous cycle of improvement and achievement. Three months after I joined, the team released the next version of the solution. A year later, it was the highest-performing team in the organization, delivering sophisticated features weekly and piloting them with doctors and patients before mass deployment. I feel immense pride in the professional level they achieved in such a short time. I remember this group fondly, who still (affectionately, I hope) call me *El Champi*.

Leading teams to high performance, guiding them in their journey to extraordinary results, is both rewarding and challenging. The main challenge is adapting one's style to meet the team or organization's needs at each moment of its continuous transformation. However, there are foundational elements, like the following set of Conscious Questions, that can serve as inspiration.

1. What new skill do we need to acquire or develop to create a world-class solution?

2. How can we achieve an early victory here?

3. How could we quickly validate this hypothesis with end customers?

4. How can I help you make this happen in minutes rather than days or weeks?

5. If this were your own money, how would you approach this differently?

6. Who has a different opinion that could help us gain new insights?

7. What are the key learnings we can take from this situation?

At the beginning of this chapter, we asked, "Why is Real Madrid such a powerful team?" My hypothesis, based on my experience, is that they achieve extraordinary results because they have had coaches who understand both People and Game Techniques. What do you think?

Exercise:

Reflect on the highest-performing work team you have been a part of. How proud are you of yourself and that team, and why? Besides the "Motivation 3.0" elements, what other factors contributed to the team's high performance?

_____

_____

_____

_____

_____

_____

Empowering teams is both a privilege and a responsibility. It is a privilege because you hold a leadership position; it is a responsibility because your words and actions must support that position. In the next chapter, I will discuss the next stage in your journey, where this privilege and responsibility transform into humility, satisfaction, and gratitude for the opportunity to invest a part of your life in your team members' lives.

Conclusion

"Effective leaders understand the importance of having with a solid framework for making decisions informed and guide others to success."

—*John C. Maxwell*

I wrote this book with a value proposition in mind. I wanted **to share a framework** with which you could create questions that mobilize people to achieve **extraordinary results**. Although I wrote this book as a hobby, I don't want to miss the opportunity to receive your feedback. I would love for you to share your opinion in the following link and comment:

1. On a scale from 1 to 10, how willing would you be to recommend this book to a colleague, family member, friend or acquaintance?

2. On a scale from 1 to 10, how much do you feel I met the value proposition?

3. Comments open.

https://www.linkedin.com/posts/
neo-bernal_agiletransformation-
agile-agilecoach-activity-
7072421252082065409-qeI5

Thank you very much for the feedback. Now that we come to the end, I would like you to vividly remember two major frameworks that emerge from the book: first, **about its structure**; and second, specifically, **about the framework**. I want you to remember three things about the *structure of the book*: **framework, training plan and examples**. Now, when it comes to the framework, have these three dimensions tattooed in your mind: **preparation, formulation and platform**.

About the Book's Structure

The framework, why is it relevant? Several years ago, during my university days, I took a test to measure my intelligence quotient (IQ). Since school I had good grades, and I felt like an academically and intellectually solid person. In fact, I studied one of my degrees with a scholarship for academic performance at one of the most reputable private universities in the city. Despite this, the test results were revealing; although my results fell within the normal range, I was very close to the lower threshold.

Looking at myself in that mirror led me to question several things: "Why did I always have the best grades if I had a low *IQ*?" «If it wasn't IQ that determined my high academic performance, what was it then? » Although I didn't have the answer immediately, it invariably came. *John Maxwell,* teacher of teachers in leadership topics, wrote in one of his books[34] that a great way to grow as a leader and influence others was through the development, use and teaching of models. These, as he explains, are simplifications of reality, which in turn facilitate the approach to complex scenarios. When I understood this, I also understood what helped me balance my lack of IQ. I remembered that the most solid and powerful knowledge I have used over the years is encoded in models, methods, and frameworks, easy for me to remember, use, and teach. If the frameworks have helped me have a privileged position in my professional career, despite my low level of *IQ*, without a doubt the **Conscious Questions** framework *will* take you to your next level of leadership.

The *training plan*, why is it key? When I combined the phrase, "Practice makes perfect," with the use of frameworks, I found that rigorous, disciplined practice makes perfect. Being rigorous and being disciplined are related concepts, but they have key differences. Being rigorous implies following a framework, model, method or framework with a meticulous and precise approach in the execution of tasks or activities. It involves a high level of attention to detail, accuracy and quality of work performed. A rigorous person strives to learn quickly from mistakes, follows established procedures, and seeks excellence in every aspect of his or her work. Rigor is associated with precision, thoroughness and strict compliance with what is established by the framework, model, method or framework.

On the other hand, being disciplined refers to having the ability to follow a set of rules, guidelines or behaviors in a constant and consistent manner, as dictated by the framework, model, method or framework. Discipline involves the will and self-motivation to stay focused on long-term goals and follow an established plan of action. A disciplined person has the ability to control his or her actions, avoid procrastination, and maintain consistency in effort toward specific goals. Discipline is related to self-regulation, persistence and willpower. In other words, discipline takes you to the gym every day at six in the morning, but rigor takes you to finish the four sets of twelve repetitions, with the most appropriate weight and movement to achieve your goals.

Why are *examples important*? The frameworks are simple, powerful, and general. Instantiating the framework, applying the mold to particular cases, adds flavor and color. We may have the perfect recipe to make the best vegan cakes in the world, but only until we implement it can we enjoy it, not the recipe, but the cake.

About the Framework

Preparation, why does it make a difference? In the words of *Jim Rohn*: "Preparation is the master key to success. If you are prepared, you don't have to worry about the future.

The formulation, why is it significant? Because it requires positive intelligence (PQ).

The platform, why is it transcendental? Because it leads you to develop a new level of consciousness.

As a leader, it is time to continue investing part of your life in the lives of others. Have you already started the training plan in chapter four? When will you do it? Who are the first three people that come to mind that you would like to give this book to? When will you do it?

Acknowledgments

I express my deepest gratitude to Almighty God, who, through my Spiritual Master, Saint Rajinder Singh Ji Maharaj, provides me with everything I need to pursue the supreme goal in this human existence.

About the Author

Juan "NEO" Bernal is an organizational performance coach specializing in adaptive management. With over twenty years of professional experience, he has participated in numerous organizational evolution processes across various industries throughout Latin America. He considers people to be the backbone of sustainable organizational evolution ("people first") and therefore dedicates most of his energy to helping individuals enhance their capabilities. Throughout these processes, he has accompanied thousands of team leaders and hundreds of C-Suite members in their leadership style transitions.

A natural entrepreneur, he has applied his knowledge and experience to his own startups. He is a co-founder of FinTechs, EduTechs, and other eCommerce companies focused on environmentally friendly products.

Over the past few years, Neo has created, refined, and/or published practical tools for working with people:

- *Ikigai Map: How to Find Your Personal Purpose*, first published at the Ágiles Latinoamérica event, Chile 2017.

- *How to Make Better Decisions Based on the Cynefin Framework*, a transcript of a conversation with Professor Dave Snowden, 2017.

- *How to Manage Organizations with Management 3.0*, a conversation with Jurgen Appelo, 2017.

- *How Agility Destroys Value*, a conversation with Fred Kofman during the Ágiles Latinoamérica event, Colombia 2022.

- *How to Accompany C-Suite Members in Their Leadership Style Transitions,* presented at ScrumDay, Colombia 2022.

His main social networks are:

Blog: https://medium.com/@jpbernalm

YouTube: https://www.youtube.com/channel/UCZiH8p-9Fw94RvgvDcuY4-Fg

LinkedIn: https://www.linkedin.com/in/neo-bernal

This is Only The Beginning...

You've reached the end of this book, but your journey doesn't stop here. Now that you've delved into the transformative power of Conscious Questions, I invite you to keep exploring, learning, and growing with Maxi, your new copilot in Leadership through **Conscious Questions**.

Maxi is an artificial intelligence trained with all the knowledge from this book, ready to support you at every step along your path. Whether you want to dive deeper into a concept, clarify questions, or apply what you've learned in your personal and professional life, Maxi will be there to help you maintain progress and keep evolving.

I asked Maxi how it can assist you, and here's what it said:

• **Suggest conscious questions:** I can formulate specific, conscious questions based on your needs or situation, helping you reflect and find answers.

- **Evaluate how conscious a question is:** I can analyze questions you have and assess their level of consciousness, providing recommendations for improvement.

- **Train in skills for asking conscious questions:** I can create personalized training plans, focusing on different types of training and skills to help you ask better questions.

- **Teach the theory behind conscious questions:** I can offer valuable information on the book's theoretical concepts, chapter summaries, practical cases, and more.

And the best part is, you can start for free:

- **5 free interactions to experience Maxi's power.**

- **7 days of free access to our monthly membership with unlimited interactions.**

- **Or take advantage of a 20% discount on our annual membership and secure a full year of support with Maxi.**

Learning doesn't have to end here. Visit our website at https://maxi.masterdragon.llc/en and continue evolving alongside Maxi.

Other Recommended Titles

Notes

1. Fernández López, Justo. 2023. " Pregunta - etimología." Hispanoteca. Accessed January 30, 2023. http://www.hispanoteca.eu/Foro/ARCHIVO-Foro/Pregunta-etimolog%C3%ADa.htm .

2. Singh, Rajinder. 2018. "How You Can Attain Spiritual Consciousness." Accessed January 30, 2023. https://www.youtube.com/watch?v=NRs_G74QD6E

3. Bernal, Juan Pablo. 2017. "The Agile Mentor is an Influencer." Medium. Accessed Jan 30, 2023. https://medium.com/@jpbernalm/el-agile-mentor-es-un-influenciador-no-solomente-un-motivador-dd55032425d4

4. Kofman, Fred. 2018. "5 Perspectives that Make You Smarter than 'Smart People 101'." LinkedIn. Published November 18, 2018. Accessed Jan 30, 2023. https://www.linkedin.com/pulse/5-perspectives-make-smart-people-101-fred-kofman/ .

5. Foundation for Critical Thinking. 2023. "Dr. Richard Paul." Accessed Jan 30, 2023. https://www.criticalthinking.org/pages/dr-richard-paul/818 .

6. Small implementation that validates a hypothesis, inspired by Agile Development, by Alistair Cockburn

7. Ries, Eric. 2011. The Lean Startup: How Today's Entrepreneurs Use Continuous Innovation to Create Radically Successful Businesses

8. Chamine, Shirzad. 2012. Positive intelligence: Why only 20% of teams and individuals reach their true potential and how you can achieve it.

9. Mehrabian, Albert. 1971. Silent Messages: Implicit Communication of Emotions and Attitudes

10. Bernal, Juan Pablo. 2018. "How to develop our maximum potential." Medium. January 3, 2018. Accessed Jan 30, 2023. https://medium.com/@jpbernalm/c%-C3%B3mo-desarrollar-nuestro-m%C3%A1ximo-potential-b7719a6fedb3

11. Science of Spirituality. 2023. "SOS - Learn Meditation." Accessed Jan 30, 2023. https://www.sos.org/meditation/learn-meditation/.

12. CBC International. 2023. Accessed Jan 30, 2023. https://cbcinternational.org/

13. Fleming, Neil D. 2001. "VARK: A Guide to Learning Styles." Accessed at http://vark-learn.com/introduction-to-vark/the-vark-modalities/

14. The Cynefin Company. 2023. "About Cynefin Framework." Accessed Jan 30, 2023. https://thecynefin.co/about-us/about-cynefin-framework/.

15. Bernal, Juan Pablo. 2023. "How to Make Better Decisions Based on Cynefin Framework." Medium. Accessed Jan 30, 2023. https://medium.com/@jpbernalm/how-to-make-better-decisions-based-on-cynefin-framework-65c16bbe7811.

16. Lieberman, Daniel Z., and Michael E. Long. 2018. The Molecule of More: How a Single Chemical in Your Brain Drives Love, Sex, and Creativity - and Will Determine the Fate of the Human Race.

17. Bernal, Juan Pablo. 2018. "How to develop our maximum potential." Medium. Published January 3, 2018. Accessed Jan 30, 2023. https://medium.com/@jpbernalm/c%-C3%B3mo-desarrollar-nuestro-m%C3%A1ximo-potencial-b7719a6fedb3

18. Bernal, Juan. "One hundred values." Medium. Accessed January 30, 2023. https://medium.com/@jpbernalm/cien-valores-7d23e77469a8

19. Tuckman, Bruce W. 1965. "Developmental Sequence in Small Groups." Psychological Bulletin 63, no. 6: 384-399.

20. Lencioni, Patrick. 2002. The Five Dysfunctions of a Team: A Leadership Fable.

21. Science of Spirituality. 2023. "About Us." Accessed January 30, 2023. https://www.sos.org/about-us/ .

22. Wikipedia. 2023. "Saiyajin." Accessed January 30, 2023. https://es.wikipedia.org/wiki/Saiyajin

23. Wikipedia. 2023. "Berserker." Accessed January 30, 2023. https://es.wikipedia.org/wiki/Berserker

24. Kahneman, D., & Tversky, A. (1979). Prospect theory: An analysis of decision under risk. Econometrica, 47(2), 263-291.

25. Kable, J.W., & Glimcher, P.W. (2009). The neurobiology of decision: consensus and controversy. Neuron, 63(6), 733-745.

26. Schultz, W. (2015). Neuronal reward and decision signals: from theories to data. Physiological reviews, 95(3), 853-951.

27. Kelley, Tom, and David Kelley. 2013. "Design Thinking." Harvard Business Review 91, no. 9: 84-92.

28. ILOSTAT. 2023. "Working Time." International Labor Organization. Accessed January 30, 2023. https://ilostat.ilo.org/es/topics/working-time/ .

29. Bernal, Juan. 2017. "How to find your purpose." Youtube. Accessed January 30, 2023. https://www.youtube.com/watch?v=Pxp6RAfWYXI

30. Alexander, Andrea, Aaron De Smet, Sarah Kleinman, and Marino Mugayar-Baldocchi. 2020. "To weather a crisis, build a network of teams." McKinsey & Company. Accessed January 30, 2023. https://www.mckinsey.com/capabilities/people-and-organizational-performance/our-insights/to-weather-a-crisis-build-a-network-of-teams

31. Pink, Daniel H. 2009. Drive: The Surprising Truth About What Motivates Us.

32. Handscomb, Christopher, and Shail Thaker. 2018. "Activate agility: the five avenues to success." McKinsey & Company. Accessed January 30, 2023. https://www.mckinsey.com/capabilities/people-and-organizational-performance/our-insights/the-organization-blog/activate-agility-get-these-five-things- right

33. Goleman, D., Boyatzis, R., & McKee, A. (2002). Primal Leadership: Realizing the Power of Emotional Intelligence. Harvard Business School Press.

34. Maxwell, John C. 2013. How Successful People Lead.

Conscious Questions
© Neo Bernal
2024

www.ingramcontent.com/pod-product-compliance
Lightning Source LLC
Chambersburg PA
CBHW031628210526
45464CB00004B/1801